BOLAND BANKERS BEHAVING BADLY

THE UNOFFICIAL STORY OF CAPITEC BANK

Published by **Hardly Read Press (Pty) Ltd**

1 2 3 10 9 8 7 6 5 4

This is a work of literary non-fiction.

Language: South African English

Type Setting: Text 9.5pt Open Sans, Header 12pt Poppins

Revised Edition, 2026: 27 May 2026

Bankers Behaving Badly with Capital and Technology was printed under ISBN 978-1-0370-2999-8. A small run of the First Edition of this book was released on 14 February 2025. This is an update to those contents and to early editions of this ISBN. In South Africa, there is currently no legal requirement to have an ISBN for electronic formats.

Print ISBN: 978-1-0370-4042-9

General Disclaimer

Facts are about what is; truth is about what it means, and the creative non-fiction writer is gifted with the opportunity to ask questions about the facts, this leading you to what they may mean, through narrative. This book is a creative retelling of facts in an imagined way. It is not authorised by, affiliated with, or endorsed by anyone. The events described are based mainly on public information, but the tone and commentary are intended for narrative and educational purposes only.

Some composite characters and scenes may be amalgamations of real-life and imagined characters or scenarios, used to make the narrative more engaging without compromising the truth. Conversations are never verbatim, but presented as retellings for educational and entertainment purposes. The author employs literary devices to present information, specific events, locations, and dialogue in an attractive, engaging, and expressive manner. While the underlying important information is nonfiction, it does not report actual events as an accurate historical account.

Neither the publisher, author, distributor, nor related parties shall be held liable or responsible for any loss or damage allegedly arising from any suggestion or information contained herein. No information is a recommendation or advice, whether legal or financial. The author reserves his right to have an opinion and to express it creatively.

This book is not a research report of any of the mentioned companies. The desire to influence the share price or misinform did not factor into telling this story. The writer has held long and short trading positions in Capitec Bank Holdings Limited at different times. To maintain integrity, **the writer does not and will not hold any position in Capitec directly or indirectly at the time of publication of this book, and agrees not to hold any positions up to 12 months after.**

Table of Contents

Preface

People often ask why I harbour such contempt for Capitec Bank, especially when the numbers appear to support the prevailing narrative. Some assume I am resentful for missing what is widely regarded as one of the most extraordinary post-apartheid share performances on the Johannesburg Stock Exchange. The truth is less flattering. I didn't merely observe Capitec's ascent from the sidelines; I actively bet against it—four times. Each wager was leveraged, and each loss left me feeling more foolish than the last. At the time, I was convinced that the market would eventually notice what I believed I was seeing. I was wrong, or at least early. The distinction matters, but it does not excuse the outcome.

I lost money, a little dignity and a great deal of confidence. The sum that disappeared into the market was not insignificant. It was enough to buy a house outright. When people suggest that my criticism is driven by bitterness, they misunderstand entirely. It is not this particular banking institution that unsettles me; it's the reflection staring back at me—the architect of my own undoing. We all find our own ways to overcome our inadequacies. I wrote this book. Is this obsessive? Indisputably so.

Criticising my use of leverage is fair. Yet fractional reserve banking is leverage institutionalised. When defaults rise or deposits fall, a bank's reserves come under pressure much like a trader facing a margin call. Banks do not drift toward failure; they accelerate once confidence breaks. It is called a "bank run" not a "bank stroll" for a reason.

Banks operate within broader economic and business cycles. Periods of economic booms are characterised by credit expansion, rising asset prices, and heightened risk-taking. As the cycle turns, these same factors can create vulnerabilities. Asset bubbles burst. Loan defaults rise, liquidity disappears.

This story is only partly about the bankers in this narrative. The Boland Bankers are no worse than any other first-generation bankers since the industry's founding. It is more about my frustration with the market's failure to recognise that banks are inherently risky, and they succeed and fail within cycles.

Bloggers, influencers, analysts, regulators, asset managers, auditors, traditional media and executives all operate within incentive structures that reward optimism and punish scepticism. Success is celebrated reflexively; dissent is often framed as hostility. When everyone is looking in the same direction, misdirection becomes effortless.

While I am generally proud to be the hippy iconoclast, I never criticise simply to fit the mould of "the barefoot contrarian." During a magic show, most of the audience is taken in by the trick, even if they know it is an illusion. I am the person who looks in the opposite direction of where you are being misdirected.

In 2013, a troubling feeling stirred in me as I scrutinised Steinhoff International's financials. Their tax rate was implausibly low, cash flow appeared far weaker than their glossy reports suggested, and their return on equity barely covered the cost of debt. Most intriguing was their peculiar knack for turning liabilities into "discontinued operations,"[1] making their BS[2] look pristine. Shareholders couldn't trust the numbers or the narrative.

When I predicted that Steinhoff's 2015 earnings per share would be heavily diluted by acquisitions,[3] much like cheap brandy at a tavern, my critique didn't go unnoticed by Steinhoff's elusive CEO. Alec Hogg[4] hinted that Jooste wanted to speak with me, probably not over coffee and an Ouma's boere beskuit. The meeting never materialised, but a word of caution did: I was wrong and should leave Steinhoff alone.

I watched Steinhoff go from R25 in 2013, to R60 the following year and then to over R90. I was beginning to doubt my suspicions, but in early December 2017, Jooste abruptly resigned from Steinhoff's board amid swirling rumours of financial impropriety. The market trembled as news broke that auditors Deloitte refused to sign off on the company's financials.

---

[1] Martin, C. (2014), *Steinhoff's drunk uncle: Distressed JD Group makes Jooste miss targets,* BizNews Available at: https://web.archive.org/web/20150709064049/http://www.biznews.com/sa-investing/2014/09/02/steinhoffs-drunk-uncle-distressed-jd-group-makes-jooste-miss-targets/ Accessed on: 19 November 2024.
Martin, C. (2014), Why Warren Buffett would never invest in Steinhoff (even if Heston Blumenthal might) Available at: https://web.archive.org/web/20170211044422/http://www.biznews.com/sa-investing/2014/09/10/warren-buffett-never-invest-steinhoff-even-heston-blumenthal-might/ Accessed on: 18 November 2024.

[2] A multi-faceted acronym that doesn't only refer to the Balance Sheet

[3] Martin, C. (2014), *Brait banks Pepkor, while Steinhoff is banking on Pepkor!,* BizNews, Available at: https://www.biznews.com/sa-investing/2014/12/02/brait-banks-pepkor-steinhoff-banking-pepkor Accessed on: 20 November 2024.

[4] The owner and editor of BizNews who kindly published most of my articles, save for the last that I submitted on Steinhoff.

This book is not an attempt to topple an institution or to profit from its misfortune. It is an attempt to understand how intelligent people, operating within accepted rules and celebrated narratives, can collectively overlook risk that is hiding in plain sight. Being right too early feels indistinguishable from being wrong. What follows is my attempt to examine why.

Prologue

A little-known short-seller, Viceroy Research, released a bombshell report on Steinhoff that ignited fierce public debate in South Africa. That report was scathing, but their next target grabbed everyone's attention. On 30 January 2018, Viceroy published "*Capitec—A Wolf in Sheep's Clothing*," aimed at South Africa's darling of the JSE and a company that had been rated the World's Best Bank by the Lafferty Group[5] in 2016: Capitec Bank.[6] Capitec has won numerous awards over the years, being the best-performing share on the Johannesburg Stock Exchange for the past two decades, achieving an average return on equity of 25% per annum.

Viceroy Research alleged that the seemingly innocent Capitec was fiercely rapacious. Their evidence evidently came from interviews with former employees, disgruntled customers, debt administrators, a plaintiff in a class action lawsuit, as well as simple mathematics revealing Capitec had overstated its gross loans by R2.5 billion to R3 billion. The trio behind Viceroy were right about the numbers not reconciling, but Fraser Perring, Gabriel Bernarde and Aidan Lau had missed a trick.

Viceroy was convinced that the only way this could make any sense was if Capitec were rolling loans or understating defaults. What

[5] A company that provides research, education, and advisory services to the banking industry worldwide.
[6] Viceroy Research (2018), A Wolf in Sheep's Clothing. Accessed at:https://viceroyresearch.org/2018/01/30/capitec-a-wolf-in-sheeps-clothing/ Accessed on: 20 July 2024.

Capitec was doing must have had their auditors' approval,[7] and Viceroy believed that it must lie in areas where there is Executive subjectivity. Although they failed to pick up on the obfuscation, you don't have to understand precisely how a trick is done to be able to know that it is still a trick. However, it would turn out that Capitec and the FSCA would insist that Viceroy explain how the trick was done. These fellows were not CFA's or CA's with the skills of Penn and Tiller.

Adding to the intrigue, in their report, Viceroy also pointed a finger at Capitec and its parent company, the PSG Group, for its ties to Steinhoff. Jannie Mouton invited the infamous CEO of Steinhoff, Markus Jooste, into the inner circle to sit on PSG Group's board. André Benjamin La Grange, father of Steinhoff's CFO, Andries Benjamin La Grange, was technically Capitec's first Executive Financial Director. He also sat on PSG's board, and his son, a substitute director for Jooste on PSG Group's board, was the CFO of Steinhoff. It would appear that La Grange and Jooste magically inflated Capitec's maiden earnings by the R3.5 million it needed,[8] and the very next day, marking the start of a new financial year, they would unwind part of the transaction. In Stellenbosch, they say, "birds of a feather drink together," and it seems these particular birds had built a very comfortable nest despite all the plausible deniability.

---

[7] PriceWaterhouse Coopers completed its last audit of Capitec in 2024 after 22 consecutive years. For 2025, KPMG and Deloitte will take over as joint auditors, with BDO handling AvaFin.
[8] See SENS published on 4 April 2002. Accessed at: https://sharedata.co.za/v2/Scripts/SENS.aspx?id=33692 Accessed on: 19 December 2024.

Under André Pierre du Plessis,[9] the Capitec CFO that we came to know, obvious paper shuffles vanished, but Du Plessis graduated from simple financial tricks to grand Copperfield-level loan book theatrics. Viceroy Research knew there was smoke and mirrors at play, but couldn't quite catch the sleight of hand.

When Viceroy's report landed, Capitec's share price dropped 23.12% intraday before recovering to close down less than 3%. Initially, the bank's executives appeared sheepish, but their swift, aggressive pushback revealed something more lupine. They commissioned a counter-report from Intellidex, although initially they tried to distance themselves from the report, but commissioned it via the Business Council. They rallied media support, and leaned heavily on regulators. Their campaign culminated in Viceroy Research being denounced in Parliament and slapped with a R50 million fine by the FSCA.[10] One couldn't help but recall Shakespeare: "The lady doth protest too much, methinks."

Capitec's resilience became more than a curiosity to me; it became an obsession. By 2025, it had defied every grim prediction. Its market capitalisation surpassed that of two traditional banking giants and an insurer combined, and was constantly jostling with Firstrand for top spot as it surpassed the R400 billion market-cap.[11] Rising stock prices have silenced critics and made sceptics doubt

[9] Andries Benjamin Le Grange was a Director from 21 July 2000 until 15 April 2002. André Pierre Du Plessis was appointed as a Director of Capitec Bank on 6 September 2001, but only stepped in as Financial Director the day after the results were released on 5 April 2002.

[10] FSCA (Financial Sector Conduct Authority). (2021) *FSCA Newsletter: September 2021, Issue 5.* Available at: https://www.fsca.co.za/tpnl/FSCA%20Newsletter %20September%202021/5.html Accessed on: 12 December 2024.

[11] Capitec's market cap exceeded that of ABSA, Nedbank and Sanlam combined, plus a few billion Rand in change.

their judgment. People want to believe in miracles and they don't like their success stories ruined.

I don't probe into the cracks in the façade to topple empires and profit from their demise. The pursuit of truth takes precedence over the pursuit of profit. Integrity and authenticity matter more to me than balance sheets and share prices. The subjects of criticism might lay some bogus charge against me as a journalist or use another scare tactic when all I am doing is attempting to highlight what I believe to be true.[12] I have a view, but I realise it is only one view, which I want to retell with as little bias as possible.

On that point, let me declare my bias upfront. I am involved in a pending court case with Capitec. Ultimately the case is about 'reckless lending', but it is my intention to cover the details of this case, as well as both Capitec's and their international company, AvaFin's association with the legal fraternity in both South Africa and Poland.

In relating the narrative of Capitec, the man at the centre of it all, Michiel Le Roux, may have opted to keep the bank ethical and honest on the surface, but he was aggressive about the legal recovery of monies owed. There is nothing illegal about that, except maybe some procedural concerns. Whether one would say that "shenanigans" were orchestrated, or you would describe these examples as "grey" accounting, the fact remains that these transactions happened. Ultimately, the bank will succeed or fail on management. In more recent years, the company managed to boost

[12] Leading media rights lawyer Dario Milo and the South African National Editors Forum (SANEF) acknowledges that this tactic is often used.

its earnings, thanks to the opaque structure of the cell-captive and then, transitioning that income directly into a bank subsidiary. Capitec might fail in the future. That is not only the nature of banking, but it is more likely when those in control have a self-interest. Banks succeed and fail for one of three reasons only.

In 2023, an Alabama family welcomed a loyal canine companion into their abode. One fateful day, tragedy struck when the beast mauled the infant in the household.[13] A sober reminder that people scoff at cries of 'wolf' when they can't see the wolf themselves, but the mistake of failing to recognise the wolf could prove costly. While the share price and company earnings continue to soar to unprecedented heights and the picture being presented is one of a meek–and-mild lamb, one would not expect to acknowledge that you might actually be dealing with a ravenous, rapacious wolf.

---

[13] Quinn, L., 2023. *Wolf hybrids are legal to own in Alabama, where the infant was fatally attacked.* People. Available at:https://people.com/legal-to-own-wolf-hybrid-alabama-infant-fatally-mauled-8410827 Accessed on: 21 September 2024.

1. Easter Sunday

The origin story of money and banking isn't so much about goldsmith IOUs and tally sticks as it is about debt records and restitution. To expect such a system to be balanced and fair to all parties would demonstrate a failure to understand the essence of fractional reserve banking. The banking system is designed to protect the banker. Not the participants in the system. Not even the bank or its shareholders.

Fractional reserve banking is a system in which banks — originally goldsmiths — keep only a portion of customer deposits in reserve and lend out substantially more. It generates revenue through credit, relying on the assumption that not all depositors will demand their funds at once.

The banker's job is to ensure that this never happens. They do this by lending to reliable people and preventing a stampede of withdrawals. Still, banks fail. When they do, it is only for one of three reasons: high loan defaults, a run on deposits, or bad management.

3 April 1994: Durban, Kwa-Zulu Natal

This is how it may have gone, that Easter weekend at a random Dutch Reformed Church[14] that ended with a familiar hymn, voices rising in perfect Afrikaans harmony. The congregation's dominee[15] stood at the church door, shaking hands with his congregation as

[14] Nederduitse Gereformeerde Kerk

[15] The title for the main minister of religion assigned to a congregation

they filed out into the autumn sunshine of 1993. Among them was a visiting dominee, Bortslap, whose onomatopoetic name made the sound of a nat klap.[16] His dog collar confirmed that he was there as a man of God, while his sharp eyes revealed that he was up to something more calculating.

South Africa was teetering on the edge of catastrophe for not embracing inclusivity. Although officially "klapping its last breath" by 1994, apartheid's ghost still haunted every institution in South Africa. The country's future was a coin toss: heads, democracy; tails, civil war. The tension was palpable, like the pause before a bar fight.

Bortslap had visited Durban over the Easter weekend the previous year. The day before that 1993 Sunday service, Chris Hani, the firebrand anti-apartheid leader, had been shot dead outside his home by naturalised Polish-born Janusz Waluś. Hani was a hero to millions, and his murder felt like a match dropped in a petrol tank.[17]

By September, the U.S. Senate had lifted economic sanctions. Weeks later, Nelson Mandela and F.W. de Klerk stood side-by-side in Oslo, accepting the Nobel Peace Prize. In a few weeks, the nation would have its first "free and fair" elections where black people could vote.

This congregation was one of the first which welcomed black workers to worship along with the white 'gemeentes.'[18] Bortslap had noted the same thing here in Durban, as in Bloemfontein: black

---

[16] Literal: wet slap (Afrikaans)

[17] Necklacing was the horrifying act of placing a tyre over a so-called political traitor's head, filling it with petrol and setting it alight as onlookers watched the person burn to death. This was initially performed by UDF members against those they saw as traitors or IFP members.

[18] NG Kerk congregations (Afrikaans)

workers were perpetually short of cash between paydays. Others had probably noted this, but chose to ignore the problem, as it didn't belong to them. He had noticed what others had noticed but chosen to ignore: black workers were perpetually short of cash between paydays. The banks regarded these loans as too small, too risky, and too administratively burdensome. Bortslap regarded them as an opportunity. He had begun to lend money to workers in his congregation and anyone else in neighbouring churches, as long as the minister would vouch for them.

"Black workers can't get loans from banks," Bortslap had said to the dominee the day before, stirring sugar into his coffee. No collateral, you understand. It's too risky, and they can't bother with the admin for tiny loans."

He pitched providing short-term loans to those congregants in need. He added fifty per cent fortnightly on first loans and forty per cent on second loans. He explained to the dominee, "These people don't understand money like we do. They live from payment to payment. Remember, the finder's fee isn't a once-off. I pay you half the original fee every time that person comes back and borrows again."

That Sunday, as the congregation dispersed, white families loaded into their bakkies and sedans, and the black families made their way to a greenbelt where they would typically have lunch before heading home. Bortslap noticed a young black lady lingering near the church steps. The dominee made eye contact with him and he nodded toward the woman. Bortslap made his way toward her, and she moved further away, allowing Bortslap to follow her until they were both out of earshot of the other churchgoers.

"Meneer?" she said, her English careful and formal. "The Dominee told me that you can help with money problems."

Bortslap looked her up and down. He knew that she worked as a cleaner for the Stein family. "Depends on the problem," he replied, glancing around to see who might be watching.

The woman's hands twisted the strap of her worn handbag. "My boys... they." Her voice cracked slightly. "I want to buy a new hat and shoes for church."

Bortslap nodded slowly. "I can help. Two hundred rand the first time. Three hundred back. Bass Stein will give me the three hundred rand. If you need more, we can talk again."

"I'm taking a risk on people banks won't touch."

She didn't consider herself to be risky. She was a church lady and would pay the money back. She nodded, unable to say anything else, and followed him toward the car.

South Africa seemed like a once-in-a-generation opportunity in 1985. Millions of black unbanked individuals were about to be presented with new economic opportunities. While sanctions had choked off other industries, South African banks had thrived in isolation, insulted from the loan losses and property crashes that battered their international peers. In the 1980s, when global banks took losses on dodgy loans and collapsing real estate markets, South African banks remained unscathed. They had fat net interest margins, steady fee income, and no competition from the international giants. With sanctions lifted, foreign investors were eager to invest, often preferring to acquire existing operations rather than start new ones.

Finance Minister Derek Keys introduced new legislation that allows banks to issue small, high-interest loans to individuals previously excluded from the formal credit system. Through the Usury Act's exemption notice of 1992, banks could charge up to 32% per annum for higher-risk small loans of less than R6,000 and for periods shorter than 36 months; however, this was insufficient to entice the established players into lending.

Mashonisas[19] charged thirty per cent per pay cycle. For decades, black people couldn't fully participate in the economy, own homes in certain areas, or start businesses. But banks were slowly beginning to open their doors—not out of charity, but because they were ready to capitalise on the higher, more attractive interest rates.

[19] Underground, informal lenders

2. Dominance Declared

9 September 1994: Lanzerac Estate, Stellenbosch

They settled into wrought-iron chairs as the estate's grandeur unfolded around them. Dutch gables caught the morning light, while the scent of lavender drifted from carefully tended gardens, mingled with the earthy aroma of Stellenbosch soil.

Le Roux,[20] a week into his appointment as managing director of Boland Bank, let his gaze drift to the mountains, a quiet smile playing on his lips as he absorbed the tranquil scene.

If life is a simulation, then some select people have been given the cheat sheets. Wiese was probably one of these people. He seemed to understand "the rules of the game" better than most.

Wiese had built a reputation as one of South Africa's most successful deal makers, a negotiator who left counterparties feeling they had won even as he walked away bagging the better end of the bargain. When deals went wrong, as several inevitably would, he proved adept at reframing the narrative.

In 1981, Wiese purchased a 42% stake in Pep Stores from his uncle for a mere R7 million. That deal gave him indirect control of Shoprite, then a modest chain of eight stores. Pep and Shoprite would go on to dominate the lower-income retail market.

---

[20] Michiel Scholtz du Pré le Roux

Christo Wiese[21] acquired 27 hectares of the sprawling luxurious wine estate, grand manor house, hotel, and antique collection from Alpha Bank curator Lieb van Jaarsveld. The price would later become the subject of allegations, denied by Wiese, that he had struck a deal at a fraction of the estate's appraised value.

"The real value", Wiese was saying, capturing his approach to deal-making, "is always what someone is willing to pay for it."

In mid-1994, whispers of irregularities in the purchase of Lanzerac reached the Sunday Rapport, which alleged Wiese had paid just one-tenth of its appraised value and another R2 million for its antiques. Public records showed a payment of R3 million by a Wiese-linked entity.[22] Incensed by accusations that he'd leveraged his influence with the SARB to secure the property below market value, according to Noseweek, Wiese sought help from the State President F.W. de Klerk,[23] to get the newspaper to print a retraction. Wiese has consistently maintained that the purchase was at arms length.

In 2012, Wiese could not refuse Markus Jooste's offer of purchase for Lanzerac. Payment was made, not in cash, but in 10 million Steinhoff International shares valued at R220 million. These would have risen to R900 million by 2016. Wiese never sold. In 2014, when Wiese sold his stake in KWV to the PSG Group, he opted to take more Steinhoff International stock.

---

[21] Christoffel F. Hendrik Wiese

[22] Wieskor Base Minerals (Pty) Ltd

[23] Wiese donated R50k of poster printing for the National Party's 1989 election campaign and de Klerk became a political ally.

In 2021, Wiese sued Jooste, alleging fraud and seeking the return of the estate. Judge Binns-Ward ruled in his favour and nullified the sale. Wiese returned the now-worthless shares and reclaimed Lanzerac in 2023, as Steinhoff entered liquidation.

Le Roux swirled the slender crystal beaker counter-clockwise, bringing it to his beaked proboscis. "A definite hint of lavender," he remarked with a playful grin, revealing slightly crooked teeth. Pretending to be oblivious to the fragrant violet-coloured bushes surrounding the manor house patio, the sparkle in his eyes betrayed his appreciation for life's simple gifts.

By contrast, Wiese leaned forward, his polished demeanour concealing a relentless drive. His overworked repertoire of self-deprecating humour made an appearance once again.

The bank, a regional favourite with a reputation for trust among ordinary South Africans, was bleeding capital. Worse still, it needed more management depth and expertise to navigate the increasingly competitive banking landscape. The 'golden opportunity' Wiese had sold to him was beginning to look like a salvage job.

Wiese's grin widened as he leaned in, his voice smooth but carrying a sharp edge. "Capital will never be a problem again," he said, his hand dropping lightly onto Le Roux's arm. Wiese's slightly curled fingers lingered as though staking a claim. Then he lifted his hand swiftly—his fingers hung in the air, along with the words: "Capital will never be a problem again." He repeated it for emphasis. The words hung in the space between them, not as reassurance but as a declaration of dominance, and Le Roux's unease deepened.

Pressing back into the chair, Le Roux extended his arms forward, fingers interlocked, palms outward. At the moment, it felt pointless explaining to Wiese that banking was about people, handshakes, trust, and helping a family have a home. A knot formed in Le Roux's stomach, his foot shifting restlessly beneath the table. He couldn't shake the feeling that Wiese's vision for Boland Bank was steering it away from what it could and should stand for.

ABSA, one of the country's largest banking groups, had already made a hostile bid for Boland. The failure of that bid was, in part, what had drawn Wiese to acquire control.

Boland's capital reserves were dangerously thin. Traditional deposit-taking was slow; an equity raise would dilute Wiese's control, which he was unwilling to do.

Wiese maintained control through a web of cross-shareholdings. The structure served his broader empire more than Boland itself — a point Le Roux was beginning to grasp.

The SARB issued licences to black-controlled banks through this period, but none would seriously challenge the established giants — a failure of transformation that would echo through South African politics for decades.

Much of the story and its characters are from the area of the Boland, and many in the tale resided in the Wilgenhof residence when they attended Stellenbosch University. Wiese is the maverick charmer—Le Roux the quiet craftsman. Also a Wilgenhof alumnus, Le Roux couldn't be more different. Where Wiese dazzles with instinct and flair, Le Roux weighs and considers. Reserved, analytical, pragmatic—Le Roux exudes the stoic discipline of a reformer, not a showman.

Many of the figures in this story passed through Wilgenhof, the Stellenbosch University residence whose alumni network would shape Afrikaner business for decades. Wiese and Le Roux both came through it, and could not have been more different.

3. Rules Explained

Banks fail for three reasons. They lend money they don't get back. Their depositors lose faith and ask for their money at the same time. Or the people running them are not up to the job. That is the entire list. It has been the entire list since 1672, when Charles II of England, broke from war, stopped paying his debts and brought down the London goldsmiths who had lent to him. The goldsmiths' depositors panicked. The withdrawals followed. The goldsmiths went under. Every banking collapse since has been a variation on that morning.

This is unusual in finance. English has a word for almost every form of taking what isn't yours — larceny, embezzlement, fraud, theft, swindle, grift — and the banking industry has lost more money than any of them. It has lost it through bad loans, panicked depositors, and bad management. You do not need to be a master criminal to rob a bank. You can simply run one badly enough.

The people who run banks understand this. Their compensation is structured around it. Bonuses are taken while the cycle is favourable. Equity is converted to cash before the reckoning. The music plays, the chairs are fewer than the players, and the people running the music know when it will stop.

These are the formal rules. They are in the Banks Act and the Basel accords and the textbooks of every business school. They explain why banks fail. They do not explain why specific banks, run by specific people, fail at specific times — or why some banks, run by specific people, are protected from failing when, by every formal measure, they probably should.

For that you need the second set of rules. In South African banking, the second set of rules is remarkably local.

Stellenbosch is a small town in the Western Cape with a university, a wine industry, and an unusual capacity to produce the people who run the country's money. The university's alumni network has shaped Afrikaner business since at least the 1940s. It has held together through political transitions that should have weakened it. Part of the reason is geographic — the town is small and the relationships formed there are dense. Part of the reason is cultural. The Afrikaner business establishment that emerged after the Second World War was built on a model of mutual support among insiders that was, in many cases, explicit policy.

The most formalised expression of the model was the Broederbond. Founded in 1918 and run in secret until its membership lists began to leak in the 1970s, the Broederbond included successive prime ministers, cabinet ministers, university rectors, newspaper editors, and the senior leadership of every major Afrikaner financial institution. Sanlam. Volkskas. Trust Bank. Rembrandt. Membership was secret. Recruitment was vetted. The stated purpose was the advancement of Afrikaner interests in every sphere of South African life, and the means by which that advancement was effected included the placing of brothers into positions where they could help other brothers. Academic work since the 1970s has documented in detail how the network shaped business appointments, government contracts, and the architecture of the Afrikaner financial sector. The Broederbond restructured in 1994 and now presents itself as a cultural organisation. The relationships it built did not restructure.

Within Stellenbosch University, certain residences mattered more than others. Wilgenhof, founded in 1903, mattered most. Its alumni included Cabinet ministers, judges, captains of industry, and a disproportionate share of the post-1990s Afrikaner business establishment. The residence operated under what its old boys described as a strong internal culture: secret rituals, an in-house disciplinary system, and a powerful expectation that what happened inside Wilgenhof stayed inside Wilgenhof. The first rule, across generations, has been described in nearly identical language: Ons praat nie uit nie. We don't speak out.[24]

---

[24] Cronje, J (2024) *'We must stand together like always!' Newly released emails show combative Markus Jooste,* News24. Accessed at: https://www.news24.com/fin24/companies/we-must-stand-together-like-always-newly-released-emails-show-combative-markus-jooste-20241224 Accessed on: 24 December 2024.

In 2024 the University of Stellenbosch commissioned an independent panel to investigate the residence. The panel was convened after university staff discovered two rooms inside Wilgenhof containing material the panel's report would describe as evidence of secret initiation practices, ritualised hierarchies, and a culture of "fear, secrecy and exclusion" sustained over many decades. The university council voted to close the residence. The Old Boys' Union contested the report and the closure. The institutional culture the panel described had been operating for over a century by then. It had produced the men who would go on to run a significant share of South African banking and business.

The men in this story come from this world. Several of them — Wiese, Le Roux, Jooste, and others — passed through Wilgenhof. They were shaped, to varying degrees, by an institution whose central organising principle was loyalty among brothers, enforced by silence. They went on to build businesses together, lend to each other's companies, sit on each other's boards, audit each other's financial statements, and vouch for each other in front of regulators and journalists. When one of them got into trouble, the others were not always neutral observers. When dissonance arose within the network, people like Jooste would remind the conflicted brother that these people are your friends, and they will look after your wife and children forever. This is not conspiracy. It is the documented structure of South African business through the late twentieth century and into the early twenty-first.

There was a fourth institution. The Dutch Reformed Church — the Nederduitse Gereformeerde Kerk — was not merely the dominant religious denomination among Afrikaners through the twentieth century. It was, for much of that period, an arm of the same establishment. Its theological faculty at Stellenbosch trained the men who led congregations across the country. Its senior leadership overlapped substantially with the Broederbond. Its synods provided theological cover for apartheid until, in 1986, the church finally acknowledged that scriptural defences of racial separation could no longer be sustained. The Truth and Reconciliation Commission's faith communities hearings in 1997 documented the church's role in the apartheid project in unsparing detail. The church itself, in the years that followed, issued apologies that did not undo what the apologies acknowledged. For the men in this story, the church was not an institution they encountered on Sundays. It was the spiritual scaffolding of the same brotherhood, the residence, the university, and the Bond had built in other registers. It was the language in which the network spoke to itself about meaning, family, and obligation.

That religious vocabulary travelled into the boardroom more often than is conventional. South African corporate culture, taken as a whole, is not notably devotional. The Stellenbosch corporate culture is an exception. AGMs and board meetings at companies in this orbit have, with some regularity, opened with prayer. Senior executives have invoked their faith in public statements, in shareholder letters, and at the lecterns of industry events. After the Steinhoff collapse, several commentators noted the dissonance between the company's devotional framing — its prayer-opened gatherings, its executives' professed values — and what the PwC investigation eventually documented. The dissonance is not best understood as hypocrisy. It is something more useful to anyone interested in governance risk: a cultural inheritance in which religious language and the language of brotherhood are interchangeable, and in which the invocation of one carries the weight of the other. When a member of this network tells you he is a man of faith, he is also telling you where he stands, who he answers to, and which obligations he considers more binding than the ones written into the company's codes.

The pattern surfaced in December 2017, in the days after Markus Jooste resigned from Steinhoff and the largest corporate fraud in South African history began to surface. Jooste's communications to his inner circle in the days that followed were eventually leaked and entered the public record. They are remarkable less for what they reveal about the fraud than for what they reveal about the network. We always stand together. The phrasing is the phrasing of brotherhood. The pact was made long before Steinhoff existed. The fraud could not have been sustained without the cooperation of a number of people across several institutions. When PwC investigated Steinhoff, the findings remained sealed for years, shrouded in silence. The loyalty that sustained the cover was not invented for Steinhoff. It was older than that.

This is the second rule of the game. The first rule says banks fail through defaults, runs, or poor management. The second rule says the people running them are members of networks that have, for generations, protected their own — and that the consequences of poor management can be deferred, redirected, or hidden for a long time when the network chooses to defend rather than expose. Both rules operate at once. The first is written down. The second is not.

A reader looking at South African banking from the outside — reading the published financials, the regulatory filings, the analyst reports — will see only the first rule. The numbers look orderly. The audit opinions are clean. The boards are appropriately constituted. The disclosures meet the standards. The bank, by every measurable indicator the reader has access to, appears to be running well.

What the reader does not see, because it is not written anywhere, is who knows whom, who owes whom, who once shared a residence in Stellenbosch with whom, and what the rules of that relationship require. The bank's solvency depends on the first rule. Its conduct, and the conduct of the people running it, depends on the second.

The chapters that follow are about the intersection of those two rules. They are about how a bank gets built by people who have known each other for decades. About how decisions get made when the formal incentive structures and the informal loyalties point in different directions. About how, when the two sets of rules eventually diverge, the cost is not borne by the network. It is borne by the depositors, the minority shareholders, the customers, and the public.

The first rule is taught in business schools. The second is taught in residences.

4. A Deal with the Devil

The summer heat of 1995 settled heavily over Boland Bank's Paarl offices. Inside, Michiel le Roux sat hunched over a legal pad, scribbling names and organisational charts as if the proper arrangement of lines and circles might conjure a miracle.

Le Roux needed help. The bank was thinly capitalised, and Wiese's appetite for deals seemed to be outpacing the bank's ability to support them. Wiese was a famously persuasive negotiator; for him, banking appeared to be a means of building influence and fortresses of power, rather than an end in itself.

A recurring pattern in Wiese's career is that he emerges from controversies — Tollgate, Steinhoff — having been, by his own account, badly served by those around him. How a dealmaker of his evident sophistication came to be so consistently distant from operational detail is a question worth holding.

In January 1995, Riaan Stassen, a fellow Stellenbosch alumnus and former "drank smouss" from Distillers Corp., came in to help. Stassen looked like someone who had spent too much time studying numbers and not enough time understanding banking.[25] Between him and Le Roux, they were as green as a Stellenbosch vineyard in spring, eager to grow but vulnerable to the elements.

[25] "drank smouss" literally alcohol hawker (Afrikaans), but they worked in the liquor industry

Wiese was already plotting his next move, his eyes glinting at the prospect of acquiring SMK Securities—a firm with a solid reputation, helmed by Jannie Mouton. Mouton only arrived in Stellenbosch later in life, having been raised in Carnarvon, in the Karoo. Mouton's rural roots seemed to ground him in a quiet self-confidence. Mouton was a man whose strategic mind combined rural pragmatism with an almost poetic ability to spot value and opportunities. He wasn't about to let Wiese waltz in and carve up the legacy he had painstakingly built.

"It's a deal with the devil," Mouton reportedly told his partners. They overruled him, and in August 1996, SMK's board of directors, voted him out of the first that he had spent thirteen years building—a brokerage that had helped arrange capital for over sixty JSE listings, most of which were oversubscribed.

At Boland, capital reserves were thinning, the Banks Act was tightening, and Wiese's pyramid structures were drawing JSE scrutiny. When African Bank entered distress in September 1995, the resemblance to Boland's own position — undercapitalised, poorly managed — was uncomfortable. NBS[26] acquired African Bank's controlling stake for R100 million.[27]

Mouton spent the next three months finding solace in reading Napoleon Hill, Warren Buffett and similar books. He had decided he no longer wanted to broker other people's deals.

[26] Natal Building Society

[27] With the assistance of BEE-partners New Africa Investments Limited (NAIL)

By November, Mouton and Chris Otto had paid ABSA R3.5 million for a half-stake in a listed shell. Mouton had spoken openly of building a South African Berkshire Hathaway.

It was a bold gamble. The company, PAG, was a struggling recruitment firm, and Mouton had no intention of dabbling in recruitment. The company's JSE ticker symbol was PSG, which would become the vehicle for forming the PSG Group, an investment juggernaut that would eventually give birth to Capitec Bank. Wiese's role in pushing Mouton out of SMK had, inadvertently, cleared the path.

Wiese's career was built on leverage — using listed structures, cross-holdings, and equity swaps and most importantly, other people's money, to control assets far larger than his direct cash investment could otherwise have reached.

From this point, Mouton would build his own platform — and, in doing so, set in motion a chain of decisions that would reshape part of South African banking.

5. Wrestling with an Angel

By mid-1996, Boland Bank was outmatched. Its branch network was modest, its reserves thin, and the country's financial giants were circling.[28] Chief among the predators was ABSA[29], a behemoth eager to assert dominance. The Articles of Association limited ABSA's stake in Boland to ten per cent, but heavyweights like the Rembrandt Group and Sanlam, who also held ten per cent each, backed ABSA, an institution in which they were also invested. With these allies, ABSA teetered on the brink of controlling nearly a third of Boland's shares.

No individual shareholder could hold more than 10%, and no matter how large their stake, they could vote no more than one per cent. This limitation insulted ABSA's Afrikaans executives, many of whom still bore scars from the Tollgate[30] scandal—a collapse from which Wiese had emerged without personal liability, to the frustration of some.

ABSA took Boland to court to challenge the restriction, but eventually withdrew the case. Boland remained vulnerable. Capital was thin and the staff had been through repeated restructurings.

---

[28] Normally referred to as rooks in the USA

[29] Amalgamated Bank of South Africa Limited

[30] A multi-billion rand fraud scheme orchestrated by the Tollgate Group in South Africa, involving the misappropriation of funds and the manipulation of financial statements. This scandal had a significant impact on the South African financial landscape, leading to the liquidation of the Tollgate Group and numerous legal proceedings. Wiese was a Director, but sold out before everything collapsed.

Amid this turbulence, Le Roux and Stassen began experimenting with an idea that ran against banking convention: running a bank like a retail store. They extended branch hours to align with customers' needs, discarding the sacred 9-to-3 traditional schedule. Bankers baulked at the expected lifestyle sacrifice. Some staff, eager to chase bonuses before moving on to competitors who respected banking hours and the lifestyle, met their lending targets somewhat recklessly. The consequence was that defaults soared, and Boland's 1996 results painted a bleak picture: Boland's loan book was unravelling.

"It's easier to lend money than to get it back," Le Roux would later say. What Boland needed was a full audit, a cleaner loan book, and fresh capital.

Wiese, however, wasn't one to let Boland flounder. His bold gambit was to create holding and operating companies and raise capital at both levels. While the Johannesburg Stock Exchange frowned upon this "pyramid" structure, it gave Wiese enormous leverage. To strengthen Boland's position, Wiese enlisted a flamboyant Malaysian businessman, Samsudin Abu Hassan, whose R270 million investment provided a crucial lifeline and preserved Wiese's control. But Samsudin's involvement was not without its consequences. His ambitions extended to New Republic Bank. Regulators baulked at the idea of a foreign investor holding significant stakes in two domestic banks. Uninterested in a merger with New Republic Bank, Wiese had no choice but to buy out Samsudin's interest in Boland, setting off a frantic search for new financing. Fortunately, a capital infusion was already being arranged.

While Wiese scrambled to secure control, a quieter figure rose within Boland's ranks. André Pierre du Plessis, a chartered accountant who had done his articles at Arthur Andersen before moving into London investment banking. He joined Boland as Head of Finance in 1996, into a bank short of strategy and capital alike.[31] Du Plessis overhauled Boland's tax structures and capital arrangements. His work helped stabilise the bank, even as Wiese's restructurings continued to reshape the wider sector.

In 1991, NBS had acquired a 20% cross-holding in Rand Merchant Bank Holdings. By 1996, the question of converting this into a full merger was on the table — but RMBH's Paul Harris was looking elsewhere. The grouping that would become FirstRand in 1998 — combining FNB, Southern Life, Momentum and RMB — was already taking shape, and NBS was not part of it.

Sensing an opportunity, Wiese made a play for NBS. Urbane, English-speaking, and deeply entrenched in the suburban mortgage market, NBS represented everything Boland wasn't. It was a tempting target.

Paul Leaf-Wright, a sartorial young executive with a flair for persuasion, helped broker the deal. Over a handshake and an exchange of ambitions, Wiese and Leaf-Wright struck a pact. Leaf-Wright convinced the NBS board to sell 25% to Boland for R220 million, and Wiese evidently promised him an executive role.[32]

---

[31] Fluent in Afrikaans, the story likes to be told of how he once exploited the linguistic similarities between his native tongue and Flemish to eavesdrop on Belgian negotiators.

[32] News24. 2005. *BoE's Leaf-Wright goes wrong*. Available at: https://www.news24.com/fin24/boes -leaf-wright-goes-wrong-20050920-2 Accessed on: 23 September 2024.

The Boland-NBS combination would carry R26.5 billion in assets. But by late 1996, the whole South African banking sector was beginning to consolidate.

6. Sour Grapes

16h00 Friday, 2 May 1997, Lanzerac, Stellenbosch, Western Cape

Le Roux was past the point of feigning amusement. It was the sixth city in as many days, and Wiese's endlessly recycled quip—"At least our worst clients aren't better off than our best shareholders"—was grating on him like sandpaper. Le Roux had an attentive focus on client service and felt like Wiese was their worst client. But, Wiese created the impression that he considered himself the best shareholder. He was in banking for access to capital.

"Enough, Christo," Le Roux said, his clipped tone mirroring his dwindling patience. "Let's get to the business at hand."

They had met at Lanzerac to discuss NBS Boland's future. They had increasingly different views of what that future should look like. For Wiese, the bank was an instrument of capital and control; for Le Roux, it was a banking business he was trying to run.

Wiese leaned back in his chair, the faintest smile playing on his lips. "What's got you worried this time, Michiel?" he asked.

Le Roux didn't bite. He'd learned early on that Wiese's disarming charm was both a weapon and shield. Instead, Le Roux outlined his concerns: Boland had previously issued convertible preference shares, half of which were now due to convert into ordinary shares. Wiese had acquired as many as he could, but the Board of Executors (BoE) held 63% of the issue — and would shortly become one of Boland's largest ordinary shareholders.

Secondly, the merged NBS Boland was about to raise another R1.2 billion in capital with selected institutions at 905 cents per share, which would further dilute shares.

Le Roux was increasingly uncomfortable with the volume and nature of loans funnelled through NBS Boland to Wiese's sprawling empire of entities. It contributed to the bank's balance sheet strain, and suspected where part of that R1.2 billion was heading. While the Banks Act allowed it, Le Roux saw the writing on the wall. International banking reforms were on the horizon, promising to shine an unflattering light on practices that, until now, had thrived in the shadows.

Le Roux proposed splitting NBS Boland into four divisions, partly to manage the sprawling operation and partly to keep closer watch on the NBS executives. The weekly Durban travel was already wearing on him. The bank was growing too fast, and he wanted to slow it down.

He felt the value of his equity stake was potentially at risk, and he had no control over the outcomes.

There's an old parable about two wolves within us: one representing greed and ego, the other humility and resolve. "Which wolf wins?" a boy asks his grandfather. The answer? "The one you feed."

For his part, Wiese had his sights set on BoE[33], whose preference shares threatened to dilute his control over Boland. A meeting with BoE's chief, Bill McAdam, was already on the calendar, and Wiese's intentions were no secret. "Institutionalise" was his buzzword, which everyone knew meant consolidating power and all his assets under one umbrella.[34]

Shortly after Wiese invited Le Roux to join him at Boland, he financed the purchase of ordinary shares in Boland with an R18 million loan. After all the changes, the NBS Boland shares were worth slightly more than R30 million. These shares were part of Le Roux's management incentive and came with "golden handcuffs." Initially, Wiese expected Le Roux to remain the managing director at Boland for a minimum period.

The two men reached a tentative agreement on what would happen to these shares and the loan. They agreed to recalculate the loan down to R14 million. Given the new agreement, Le Roux intended to sell his Boland Bank shares to pay back the R14 million, leaving him with just over R16 million in cash.[35] But, as far as Wiese was concerned, these shares had not vested, and the handshake deal,

---

[33] Board of Executors. BoE was founded in 1838 as a trust company administering estates, but in recent years had expanded into private and merchant banking, asset management and insurance. The company listed on the JSE in 1987 with Bill McAdam at the helm and now had assets under management of R1.5 billion and attributable earnings of R1.7 million.

[34] This was an early version of what Wiese would claim to be doing with Steinhoff International, and we can learn from Wiese's playbook a little about what his actual intentions might have been with Steinhoff by following what he did with BoE.

[35] IOL. (2000) 'Court asked to dismiss Wiese's case'. Available at: https://www.iol.co.za/business-report/economy/court-asked-to-dismiss-wieses-case-775075 Accessed on: 10 November 2024.

like so many in Wiese's career, came with invisible fine print—Le Roux could not sell the shares yet.

By the time the last of the Pinotage had drained from their glasses, their tension had reached a quiet boil. As the shadows lengthened in that dimly lit room, it was clear that their relationship had transformed from partners to something else entirely: adversaries bound by a fragile alliance.

Le Roux left the meeting with a meticulously sketched plan to safeguard his vision for NBS Boland, as well as his name and equity stake. Yet, as he walked to his car, the plan felt vulnerable to the relentless waves of Wiese's ambition. The handshake deal, which had seemed so quaintly pragmatic at the moment, began to unravel under its vagueness. Years later, the fallout from these moments would ripple through the courts and among the Stellenbosch community.

Le Roux's journey into banking had been motivated by good intentions—to build something sustainable, improve customer service, and make money. But he wasn't blind to the fact that he'd partnered with someone who loved deals more than banking. Wiese wasn't in it for the long game; he thrived on the adrenaline of acquisitions, leveraging assets to wield influence. And while Le Roux had started believing they shared a vision, he now realised that Wiese's appetite for risk was insatiable.

Le Roux was beginning to doubt he would ever see the returns he had been promised. The equity stake that had drawn him in now felt more like a leash. He was already thinking about what came next.

7. 'n Boer Maak 'n Plan[36]

Jannie Mouton had a talent for turning setbacks into beginnings. Fired from SMK in 1995, he spent three months reading and planning before returning to the market on his own terms.

In 1996, PSG Group took its first giant leap with a rights issue through SBS Warburg, which later became UBS,[37] inflating its capital to R21 million—triple the original valuation when Mouton and Chris Otto had acquired it from ABSA. It was classic Mouton: pragmatic enough to see the opportunity, audacious enough to grab it.

Eighteen months later, Mouton sold PAG's operating assets to Educor for R107 million, leaving PSG as a cash shell again — a clean platform for what came next.

With cash in hand Mouton returned to stockbroking with a smaller operation, pulling in a few loyalists from his SMK days[38] PSG Online would become one of South Africa's first online trading platforms.[39] This venture reflected Mouton's ability to spot trends before they became mainstream.

By 1997, the Asian Financial Crisis had shaken markets. The JSE allowed cash shells to remain listed for six months while they sought

---

[36] A farmer (Afrikaaner) makes a plan (Afrikaans)

[37] Union Bank of Switzerland (not to be confused with United Building Society which become one of the banks that merged into ABSA in the early 1990's)

[38] Jaap du Toit and Johan van der Westhuizen, inter alia.

[39] Many traders opened their PSG Online accounts by entering Moneyweb's Make-a-Million share trading competition which had a first prize of R1 million for the best trader.

new operating assets to reverse into them — giving acquirers access to listed status, a shareholder base, and the ability to issue equity.[40]

One cash shell wouldn't be enough to achieve Mouton's ambitions. Enter Servgro, a listed cash shell with potential. Ever the opportunist, Mouton approached his former boss,[41] and spokesman for Servgro, Peet van der Walt, with a bold plan: inject PSG Financial Services into Servgro. Van der Walt agreed, and soon, a deal worth R863 million gave PSG Group a 61.9% stake in the newly minted PSG Financial Services.

Not content with this coup, Mouton also engineered an early Black Economic Empowerment transaction, issuing 10 million shares to Siphumele Investments. Between the Servgro reversal and the BEE deal, PSG's net asset value per share rose from 147 cents in 1997 to 617 cents in 1998.[42]

By 1998, PSG Nobel Capital, a private equity company, was also listed, raising R1.2 billion. The establishment of PSG Investment Bank soon followed. But Mouton's crowning glory came from an unassuming idea: Capitec Bank. What began as a low-cost banking solution for underserved communities evolved into South Africa's most consistently profitable bank.

It didn't take long to prove Mouton right about not selling SMK to Boland. Later, NBS Boland would merge with the BoE, which owned the stock brokerage Ed Hern. The two entities would form BoE

[40] an issue of shares offered at a special price by a company to its existing shareholders in proportion to their holding of old shares.
[41] When at Federale Volksbeleggings
[42] Mouton, J (2011), "and then they fired me", Tafelberg, p83

Securities. Nedcor absorbed BoE in 2002, following the A2 banking crisis, and BoE Securities would become part of Nedcor Securities. Mouton's ex-SMK partners[43] were left clutching little more than empty promises and nostalgic regrets. His journey from a fired executive to the architect of a financial empire was a masterclass in turning adversity into opportunity. He didn't just build a company; he reimagined the game's rules. Like a maestro conducting an orchestra, Mouton knew how to wield listed equity to attract capital, make acquisitions, and create value.

---

[43] Kitshof and Senekal

8. Financial Integrity

The unregulated, lucrative world of microlending was turning into a gold rush when Trevor Manuel raised the limit from R6,000 to R10,000 for loans with larger-than-normal interest rates. While traditional banks turned their noses up at small loans to lower-income earners, cash loan shops pounced, charging eye-watering interest rates.

Enter Koos Brand, a former car dealership MD turned entrepreneur who sought a middle path: loans priced higher than banks but cheaper than the predatory loan sharks. His timing was impeccable. Public sector workers, such as teachers, had stable incomes but often needed access to credit. Brand offered them loans, but quickly burned through its capital and struggled with the technology and infrastructure. He needed a partner, and Boland Bank, already dabbling in small-scale agricultural lending, saw the potential.

Boland bought into Brand's business and scaled it with a game-changing twist: obtain repayment via the government payroll system, Persal. With repayment effectively guaranteed at source, the bank could offer larger loans on longer terms — some up to 48 months.

As the Persal-backed book grew, a problem emerged inside Boland's microlending operation: the bank's internal accounting records were not reconciling with the statements it was sending to customers.

As per Wiese's plan to "institutionalise" his assets, over 1997 and 1998, a series of transactions culminated in the merger of BoE and NBS Boland — a group with R80 billion in assets, then the third-largest South African bank by market capitalisation. The new company still owned African Bank and had a 20% interest in Rand Merchant Bank, but now included Wiese's 38% in Monex and 20% in Pepkor. Pepkor held an interest in listed entities such as Shoprite and Tradehold. It also had its trade assets, such as Pep Stores and Ackermans. BoE now had R3.5 billion in free cash, excluding the R500 million they were about to get from Old Mutual. Wiese, CFC, and BoE executives retained control through a web of pyramid structures and shares with different voting rights (N-class), limiting the influence of minority shareholders.

Chris Oosthuizen, who later became a founding director at Capitec Bank, started at Boland Bank in 1976. He had extensive practical experience rolling out banking systems from scratch and was responsible for the IT system that would eventually manage the administration of the microlending division.

Bank Windhoek was founded by a group of local Namibian entrepreneurs led by Koos Brandt. To get the bank off the ground with an established footprint, the group negotiated the takeover of eight local branches of Volkskas Bank in 1990 and then partnered with Boland Bank to maintain them. Oosthuizen flew to Namibia and spent several months with a team, ensuring everything was operational.

The microlending book had reconciliation problems. It is unclear how widely understood these problems were within the bank, but some think that Oosthuizen and other insiders were likely aware that the software system they used for the microlending book had problems. Accounts continued accruing interest after being written off or sent to collections, and the book's true value was difficult to determine. Boland nonetheless carried it at a nominal R872 million and was actively seeking a buyer.

Enter the Theta Group, listed on the JSE, helmed by Leon Kirkinis, a man with ambitions as big as his appetite for risk, but usually found wearing jeans, a golf shirt, and sneakers. By September 1997, Theta had acquired controlling interests in several financial entities, including Alternative Finance, King Finance, and Unity Financial Services, which were later consolidated into its operations. Theta's ambition was to expand its footprint within the microlending segment, and it already had a network of approximately 100 branches, which it sought to further develop. NAIL[44] shareholders in Theta Group had also acquired a stake in African Bank with NBS. Now, Kirkinis was interested in purchasing the remainder of African Bank, which included the brand, banking license, and loan book from BoE. During the negotiation process, Wiese made Kirkinis an offer that was hard to refuse.

Behind the scenes, Wiese was also busy orchestrating the financing for Theta's purchase. He had agreed to reportedly sell R500 million of Pepgro shares to Old Mutual, and BoE had evidently decided to lend Theta R500 million to purchase the book. Not only was Wiese offering Kirkinis a loan book for 57 cents in the rand, but he had

[44] New Africa Investments Limited, a black economic investment company on the JSE.

essentially arranged the finance for him upfront—— on the face of it, a favourable deal.

Theta inserted a profit warranty: Boland PKS guaranteed an after-tax profit of R167 million by September 1999, with a 20:1 penalty clause that could materially affect Boland's earnings. Critics would later describe the transaction as Boland offloading a problem book onto a buyer not yet equipped to assess it.

The transactions completed in 1998; Theta rebranded as African Bank Investments Limited the following year. What had been sold as an opportunity would prove harder to manage than the buyer anticipated.

A particularly alarming discovery was that the existing provisions for bad debts in this loan book were insufficient. There was a material discrepancy between the bank's internal accounting records and the actual risk profile of its loan portfolio. The provisions did not accurately reflect the expected losses, implying a significant overstatement of the book's value. Theta had overpaid for the book, but they still didn't know by how much.

Theta's management struggled to reconcile a particular section of the book they had purchased — more than seven thousand accounts. Gawie Cillie, by the accounts of those who worked with him, spent months trying to unravel it and could not. The errors were not in African Bank's favour. Boland had overstated the values, and Theta knew by then that the R167 million warranty would not be met.[45]

When Theta purchased African Bank, BoE initially received a 35% stake, which had to be whittled down to 17.4% to compensate for failed profit warranties. When BoE eventually sold its remaining holdings in African Bank Investments Limited (ABIL), it showed a non-headline loss of R716 million.

A question follows from the foregoing: how did a loan book that the bank's own employees could not reconcile pass external audit? Deloitte was the auditor of Boland, of Theta Group, and later of African Bank — and the question of whether common auditors across both sides of a transaction can fully discharge their independence obligations is one the profession has wrestled with for decades. The discrepancies in the loan book were not clerical. They represented a meaningful gap between the reported numbers and the underlying reality.

If the issues in the Boland book did not surface in audit, what mechanism would catch them next time?

Either the systems were inadequate to the task — in which case the bank's reporting was unreliable — or the systems were adequate and the values had been deliberately overstated. Neither possibility was reassuring. The financial system depends on its gatekeepers — auditors, regulators, and executives. When any of them fall short,

[45] Welz, M (2000), BoE Gets A Boland Hangover, Noseweek. Accessed at: https://noseweek.co.za/wp/article/boe-gets-a-boland-hangover/ Accessed on: 14 Dec 2024

whether through inattention or worse, the cost is borne by everyone downstream[46]

The book's irreconcilability was not a clerical anomaly. It reflected real issues in valuation and reporting — issues that, in any banking institution, sit at the foundation of sound operations.

[46] Daily Maverick. (2020) 'Deloitte accuses key Irba witness of "lies" at African Bank disciplinary hearing'. Available at:https://www.dailymaverick.co.za/article/2020-06-16-deloitte-accuses-key-irba-witness-of-lies-at-african-bank-disciplinary-hearing-part-two/ Accessed on: 10 June 2024

9. Legion of Misfits

The seven executives who transitioned from Boland Bank to establish Capitec Bank were later dubbed the "dream team" by staff members. However, in 1999, these executives appeared more like " a demonic nightmare" to Tom Boardman, the chief executive of BoE, who would eventually seek to expel this legion of misfits.

Boardman initiated an investigation into Boland PKS's governance practices. The investigation scrutinised Riaan Stassen, André du Plessis, and Michiel le Roux. Stassen informed the media that the inquiry pertained to a property deal and no irregularities had occurred. Still, Tom Boardman's statements suggested otherwise.[47] Already dissatisfied with the turn of events and now facing mounting pressure, Michiel Le Roux opted to resign.

"As jy nie kan vat nie, moet jy padgee" — "If you can't take it, step aside" — was the essence of Wiese's reply. The line cut deeper than Wiese seemed to realise.He had invested immense energy into transforming Boland into a nimble, successful small bank, only to see his efforts undermined as he watched Wiese repeatedly draw on it for capital, acquisitions, and restructuring across his broader empire.

Le Roux realised that soon, no one would have the keys to unlock the golden handcuffs, and bonuses were less likely with Boardman

[47] Mail & Guardian, (2000, 28 April). Boland Executives Resign, Available at: https://mg.co.za/article/2000-04-28-boland-executives-resign/ Accessed: 4 Jan 2024,

and the BoE board pulling the strings. For all his toil, it was evident that Le Roux was angry.

Perhaps sensing their heads were next on the chopping block or motivated by what they had witnessed in the treatment of Le Roux, according to Noseweek, the top eight Boland PKS management cunningly granted themselves undisclosed bonuses totalling R10 million (after tax) without BoE's approval. Director Riaan Stassen received a substantial bonus of R2.3 million.

André Olivier, a colleague of André du Plessis from Arthur Andersen, was brought in to support the financial department in 1996. Christian van Schalkwyk, a BCom and LLB graduate who became a CA (SA), briefly served as a tax consultant at Arthur Andersen before spending a decade as an attorney. He joined Boland Bank in 1997 to head credit risk and legal services. Carl Fisher, a marketing executive from Distell, joined in 1997. Du Plessis, Olivier, Van Schalkwyk and Fisher awarded themselves tidy bonuses ranging between R250,000 and R400,000 each. Chris Oosthuizen, who led IT, reportedly received R600,000. These after-tax bonuses paid to Boland executives were kept secret from BoE shareholders and executives at the time.[48] Stassen later claimed that BoE had accepted Boland's independence and non-interference in its management. Evidently Boardman saw it differently and was determined to dismantle Boland's structure entirely.

The group of six—Riaan Stassen, Chris Oosthuizen, André Olivier, André Du Plessis, Carl Fisher, and Christiaan van Schalkwyk—soon

---

[48] Welz, M. (2000), 'BoE gets a Boland Hangoever', Noseweek, Issue 28, Available at: https://noseweek.co.za/wp/article/boe-gets-a-boland-hangover/ Accessed on: 14 Decr 2024

followed Le Roux and resigned, taking a four-month sabbatical. Some claim they were "nudged to leave," while others agree that the situation had become untenable. André du Plessis described the working conditions as unbearable.[49] During their sabbatical, sustained by the bonuses from Boland, the group conceptualised the idea that would eventually give birth to Capitec.

The pattern of executive remuneration at Capitec — non-negotiable bonuses, regardless of shareholder pushback — would surface repeatedly in the years that followed.

A more recent example of this "entitled" culture occurred in 2021 when more than 51% of Capitec's shareholders voted against the non-binding resolution on the group's implementation report. The Remuneration Committee responded by determining that the 2018 Share Appreciation Rights and options, for which the performance period ended during the year under review, would be vested based on pre-COVID-19 performance metrics.[50] This decision effectively shielded the executives from financial consequences, allowing them to maintain their bonus payouts despite shareholder disapproval.

The pattern, illustrated in 2021 and visible elsewhere, is one of adjusting performance metrics in ways that protected executive payouts. It is an instance of what is sometimes called the Texas Sharpshooter Fallacy — drawing the target around the shots already fired.

[49] As quoted from "Masters Of Money - Strategies For Success From The CFOs Of South Africa's Biggest Companies" by KC Rottok Chesaina

[50] Moneyweb (2022), *Capitec under fire – again – for its executive pay,* Accessed at: https://www.moneyweb.co.za/news/companies-and-deals/capitec-under-fire-again-for-its-executive-pay/ Accessed on 24 September 2024.

Taking bonuses despite missed targets, or retrospectively shifting the targets to ensure payment, signals priorities: it tells shareholders and employees what the system is for, and who it is for.

10. Reluctant Banker

"No bank in the world, no matter how strong, can withstand the kind of publicity and unfounded smear campaign we have suffered,"[51] said Wiese's old business partner, Dato' Samsudin Abu Hassan, in early 1999.

Samsudin still owned 75% of NRB through SMG Holdings. When reports of the bank's troubles surfaced, depositors withdrew rapidly, triggering a liquidity crisis. NRB passed first to Saambou and then to PSG Investment Bank; Samsudin's South African banking career was over.[52]

Benjamin Franklin once said, "A great empire, like a great cake, is most easily diminished at the edges." Boland PKS had grown beyond what Wiese had originally acquired. It was also now vulnerable to failure.

At 3 a.m. on February 21, 2000, journalist Deon Basson sent his draft report on BoE to their PR consultant. Wiese phoned within hours. By the following morning, Wiese was at breakfast across from Basson and BoE executives, objecting to a headline that suggested he regretted having entered banking, and to the report's implication that he was over-indebted.

Wiese defended Boland's record since his acquisition, while passing lightly over the debt he had taken on to acquire control. He valued

---

[51] Schoonakker, B (1999), *I'm not broke, says Samsudin after fiasco,* Accessed at: https://mahazalimz.tripod.com/130799xc.html Accessed on: 12 December 2024

[52] Mail & Guardian (1999), *Who Looks After Your Bank?* Accessed at: https://mg.co.za/article/1999-03-12-who-looks-after-your-bank/ Accessed on: 12 Dec 2024

properties like Monex and Century City at over R300 million — valuations Basson described as inconsistent with what was publicly known about the assets. Basson, in his own later account, characterised the meeting as a mix of legal posturing and pressure.[53]

The Monex story began with Ilco Homes, a company in financial distress. Accounts of how Wiese acquired the controlling stake — reportedly for R76 — differ. One version describes a forced acquisition, with the threat of withdrawing a R30 million overdraft used to apply pressure.[54] Another holds that Ilco's repayment difficulties were genuine and the transfer of control was the lender's reasonable response. What is documented is that Boland Bank funded Wiese's subsequent rezoning of the land for a casino and entertainment complex.[55]

Wiese's career was built on leverage — using listed structures, cross-holdings, and equity swaps to control assets far larger than his direct cash investment.

Pepkor's[56] ownership history illustrates the point. Wiese listed Pepkor in 1988 with a dual share structure that preserved his control. In 1999, he sold a substantial stake to BoE; he reacquired exposure to the business in 2004 through transactions involving Old Mutual and Brait. In 2011, Brait acquired 24.6% of Pepkor for R4.2 billion in cash, with a further 10.3% via a special-purpose vehicle for

---

[53] This is a retelling from an article of Deon Basson's that appeared in the Finance Week, in early March 2000.

[54] Welz, M. (2000), 'Christ Wiese's Steal Deal', Noseweek, Issue 13, Available at: https://noseweek.co.za/wp/article/christo-wieses-steal-deal/ Accessed on: 25 June 2024.

[55] Wingate-Pearse, G. (2007) Century City hot today, Moneyweb, Accessed at: https://moneyweb.co.za/archive/century-city-hot-today/ Accessed on: 25 June 2024.

[56] Pepkor Holdings Limited

R671 million. In November 2014, Steinhoff announced it would acquire 92.3% of Pepkor — 52.47% from Wiese's Titan Investments and Thibault Square Financial Services, in exchange for 609.1 million Steinhoff shares at R57 each, and 37.06% from Brait, for R15 billion in cash plus 200 million Steinhoff shares.

Following Steinhoff's collapse in 2017, Wiese pursued litigation to recover what he could. By 2022, he again held influence at Pepkor — 21.3% of the shares and 44.3% of the voting rights. At Shoprite, he holds 11.6% of the equity and 32.2% of the votes. The pattern, throughout, has been controlled through voting structure rather than majority equity ownership.

Christo Wiese's final act in banking was a pragmatic retreat. In late 1999, he resigned as Director. BoE then sold its stake in Pepgro back to Wiese, who focused on his retail ventures. PEP Bank, a subsidiary of BoE, became a stopgap, allowing BoE to offer basic financial products to Pepkor customers. Left with Century City and Monex, BoE struggled to salvage their value, managing only to stabilise the Canal Walk shopping centre. Eventually, Monex liquidated.

Wiese didn't linger in banking. Although the venture might have appeared to be a failure, in terms of his personal balance sheet, he was wealthier at the turn of the millennium than he had been when he first entered banking six years earlier. Now, Christo Wiese's focus was back where he started—diamonds.

As a young man, he took a chance on a diamond mine, Octha Diamonds—risky by any measure—and later flipped it back to the

Ruperts at a healthy profit — reportedly sold for R300 million. Octha was where Wiese first met Markus Jooste.

A favourite Wiese anecdote concerns a dinner party he hosted at the aptly named On the Rocks. He served doughnuts for dessert, announcing that three contained diamonds. The "diamonds," it turned out, were zirconias bought for less than R40. The drama — including, reportedly, the next morning's bathroom searches — became part of the Wiese mythology.[57] Now, he was leveraging a stake in Ocean Diamond Mining (ODM) to drive up its share price during a takeover battle. At least that is evidently how Remgro perceived it. It wasn't ultimately about mining; it was about leveraging assets.

The banking sector around Wiese was consolidating under liquidity pressure. PSG Group, under Mouton, was beginning to look at the microlending sector. Le Roux — Wiese's former collaborator — had joined PSG and was assessing its nascent microlending operations. He would later say that Wiese's exit from banking added to his determination to demonstrate that his own departure from Boland had not been a reflection on his abilities.

Wiese described his motivation for selling Pepkor and other assets to BoE as "internationalising" his portfolio. In practice, he had also offloaded several of his weakest assets — Monex, Century City, Boland Bank, and the stake in African Bank — onto BoE's balance sheet. BoE never recovered, and was absorbed by Nedcor during the small-banks crisis of 2002.

---

[57] Strydom, TJ (2019), *Christo Wiese: Risk & Riches*, Tafelberg p51-52.

11. Withdrawal Symptoms

Thursday, June 24, 1999: 23h55

The beeping woke him in the dark chill of winter, the sound pulling him from an uneasy sleep. He hit snooze, granting himself fifteen more minutes before facing what he knew would be a long night. Friday paydays were always chaotic—lines at the ATMs stretched long and tense. Kobus wasn't just a branch manager at one of PSG Smartfin's cash shops; he was its anchor, responsible for keeping operations running.

Friday paydays were emblematic of his world. The money had dropped into accounts just after midnight, and by 12:30, he stood at an ATM, flanked by a police Sergeant, a uniformed insurance policy against robbery. The policeman, ever willing, pocketed the extra cash Kobus paid him for his time. For Kobus, it was money well spent—PSG Smartfin had no insurance to cover stolen funds, and any theft would leave him explaining himself to over a hundred irate borrowers.

Kobus wore a thick coat modified with sewn-in pockets to store cash efficiently. Inside, he secured bundles of ATM cards with rubber bands. The system was rudimentary: they scrawled each borrower's card and PIN onto slips of lined paper. He'd pull a card, punch the PIN into the ATM, withdraw the maximum amount, and tuck the cash into his pocket alongside the receipt. The process was slow, deliberate, and mind-numbing, stretching into five-hour marathons as his gloveless fingers worked against the cold.

By dawn, Kobus was back at the shop, sorting cash and preparing deposits for the day. Borrowers queued outside, anxious to reclaim their cards and make essential purchases. Many would return days later to hand the cards back for another loan, trapped in a borrowing cycle that mirrored the predatory efficiency of the system itself. He saw their tired faces and knew their stories—parents trying to buy food, spaza shop owners desperate to keep shelves stocked, and workers caught in a loop where survival came at a thirty per cent cost.

The payday loans were straightforward: thirty per cent interest, whether you borrowed for a few days, a week, or a month—never longer than until your next payday. Once a borrower had received two consecutive loans, they needed to take a "payday loan holiday" before being allowed to return to the debt cycle.

"Bloody loan sharks, the lot of you," the Sergeant muttered, watching Kobus bundle up another stack of ATM cards. His words hung in the air, more observation than accusation.

Kobus shrugged it off, but the words lingered. He wasn't getting rich. He was working long nights, counting cash that wasn't his, watching as owners far removed from these cold streets raked in profits built on his sweat and the borrowers' desperation.

When Jannie Mouton invited Michiel le Roux to evaluate PSG's microlending operations, he wanted him to experience the world of payday theatre. Le Roux's reaction was immediate and visceral.

"This is not the kind of business I want to be involved in," Le Roux told Mouton.

Mouton pressed. "Johann Rupert told me I was exploiting the poor before the entire Remgro board. You probably think the same?"[58] Le Roux had been in banking but didn't feel good about the exploitative interest rates on some of these loans.

Undeterred, Mouton's response was along the lines of: "We're giving people access to finance they wouldn't otherwise get. These loans let spaza shop owners turn over stock five or six times before they pay us back. It's high risk, sure, but it creates opportunity. Come see for yourself."

Le Roux reports that what struck him from his branch visits with Chris Otto was the dignity PSG afforded its clients—an unexpected contrast to the cold indifference of larger banks. Borrowers weren't just reduced to numbers; they were people with names, stories, and hopes. The "dignity" framing is harder to sustain when the same operation charges thirty per cent per month — or part thereof — on a loan.

---

[58] Mouton, J (2011), "and then they fired me", Tafelberg

By the turn of the century, sixteen million economically active South Africans navigated a world where traditional banks controlled credit, leaving the underserved vulnerable to short-term, high-interest loans. PSG Smartfin's opportunity was to position itself at the intersection of necessity and profit.

Lourens Van Zyl and Werner du Plessis pitched their payroll deduction model to Mouton, who initially dismissed it. "I don't want to profit from getting people into debt," he said. However, persistent persuasion led to PSG acquiring a handful of branches, rebranding them as PSG Smartfin, and merging them with Finaid Financial Services, another short-term lender founded by Bortslap[59]. By June 1999, PSG had added PSG Anchor Finance, a business specialising in longer-term loans through payroll deductions, to the mix.

The payroll model was ingenious. Loans were deducted directly from salaries, reducing default risk and increasing profitability. However, it wasn't without cost—brokers took hefty commissions for securing clients, and the process demanded constant cash management.

Le Roux eventually agreed to conduct due diligence on PSG's microlending ventures. What he found surprised him. Beneath the surface of high-interest loans lay an ecosystem of small businesses and individual borrowers who relied on the system to sustain their livelihoods. The narrative Le Roux was selling was that while the system wasn't perfect, it wasn't entirely predatory either.

[59] In this instance we are referring to Cornelius 'Neels' Johannes Borstlap

When Le Roux was ready to step in, PSG's cash shops had expanded to 60 branches. What began as a system of midnight withdrawals and rubber-banded ATM cards transformed into a streamlined operation. Bortslap, an NG Kerk dominee, was initially earmarked to run the merged entity.

Bortslap's success owed much to tapping into the church network of dominees,[60] deacons, and farmers, all confident that "god-fearing" folk would let their consciences nudge them into repaying loans on time. Outsiders might call it peer pressure, but for the faithful, it was divine proof that helping fellow believers paid off—literally.

Bortslap had been building a nice network of Finaid branches in the Free State and Kwa-Zulu Natal, and to say that he was disappointed that Le Roux didn't find him to be the obvious choice for leading what would soon become a bank for the unbanked would probably be an understatement.

Bortslap had shares and a directorship, but he believed he should have been the managing director. Bortslap would resign from the board on 6 October 2004 with 320,322 ordinary shares, which were trading at approximately R9.30 per share at the time. That would make his stake worth roughly R2.9 million. That same stake today would be worth over R1.6 billion at the time of writing. Unfortunately, Bortslap sold his shares.

[60] a minister or pastor in the Dutch Reformed Church

12. Building Plans

For Le Roux, the early work of building a bank was unglamorous. It was about laying foundations, one decision at a time.

South Africa's microlending sector at the time was lightly regulated and rapidly growing. Salaried workers, carrying loans alongside funeral policies and insurance premiums, often had little left after payday — and as the debts compounded, the cost of the borrowing became apparent. PSG's payroll deduction business, Anchor Finance, was at the harder edge of this market. Brokers earned commissions of up to 15%, with incentives tied to the volume of debt sold rather than to borrower outcomes.

Le Roux found the brokers and their incentives troubling. The numbers reflected the dysfunction: Anchor Finance posted a R363,000 loss in 1999. The business as structured was not sustainable.

Le Roux saw an opportunity to do things differently — to build a bank that did not require taking customers' ATM cards and PINs as effective security. He agreed to join PSG, with the aim of building something new rather than patching the existing model.

Le Roux acquired a shelf company, Business Venture Investments No. 285, and renamed it PSG Specialised Lending. PSG's microlenders — Anchor Finance, Finaid Financial Services, and Smartfin Financial Services — were merged under a single umbrella,

Keymatrix. The Keymatrix name reflected Le Roux's belief that systems and technology would shape the future of lending.

Transforming the business would require more than just his efforts. So, Le Roux reached out to trusted allies, including Riaan Stassen. Initially hesitant to leave Boland PKS for what was, at the time, essentially a start-up, Stassen's reluctance mirrored a common internal struggle: the pull between security and the unknown.

By the end of 1999, PSG Specialised Lending had shed its start-up status. Advances surged from R21 million to R84 million, and profits reached R6.9 million. The business doubled its footprint to 120 branches and expanded its workforce to over 460 employees across South Africa, Namibia, and Botswana. Yet despite these milestones, Le Roux remained restless. Payroll loans—long-term, high-commission products—didn't align with his vision for a bank that served people's real needs.

In 2000, Le Roux sold Anchor Finance to Unifer for R26 million, exiting the payroll deduction sector. The timing proved fortunate: Unifer would later collapse in the small-banks crisis. The sale freed capital for Le Roux to focus on building a full-service bank.

The company needed a name. Mouton and Chris Otto briefly considered modelling on Grameen Bank; they also considered "Prosimian" (after the lemur-like primates) before settling on Keynes Rational — a nod to John Maynard Keynes. Keynes Rational became the holding company; Keymatrix housed the operating businesses.

At the turn of the century, South Africa's major banks were cautious about the mass market. BoE's PEP Bank contributed less than half a per cent to its earnings. Leon Kirkinis, founder of Theta and now heading African Bank, focused solely on microlending. Other major banks dabbled, but none had committed fully. Saambou, for instance, ventured into micro-lending through acquisitions but struggled to integrate these businesses seamlessly.

In contrast, Le Roux was building something coherent. His vision was not of a fragmented microlender but a holistic banking solution — a place where customers could deposit their salaries, manage their finances, and access credit without exploitation. This vision was rooted in balancing the practicalities of finance and the ethical responsibility of serving people.

Gerrie Fourie had worked at Stellenbosch Farmer's Winery (which merged with Distillers Corporation after Le Roux had left); the two men had not previously met. On the recommendation of Le Roux's former colleagues, Fourie joined Keymatrix to lead it.

Gerrie Fourie joined Keymatrix in April 2000, just as the pieces fell into place. Profits surged fourfold from R1.2 million to R9.8 million. The number of branches doubled, and the workforce expanded significantly. The expansion wasn't just about numbers but about presence—about being there for communities in South Africa, Namibia, and Botswana.

Le Roux's story is that he seized the opportunity when he heard that the group of six executives left BoE en masse in mid-2000. The narrative that makes sense to me is that Stassen and Le Roux had been communicating before their walkout. It might have been a surprise for Fourie to hear that Stassen was joining, but Le Roux was crafting a plan to build a bank, and I think he was less surprised.[61]

Now, all Le Roux needed was the banking licence to build the infrastructure necessary for deposit-taking and transform the micro-lender into a fully-fledged bank.

[61] Retief (2023), Netwerk24, Hanlie gesels met Mnr. Capitec: SA is propvol geleenthede, Accessed at: https://www.netwerk24.com/netwerk24/stemme/profiele/hanlie-gesels-met-mnr-capitec-sa-is-propvol-geleenthede-20230709 Accessed on: 13 September 2024

13. Listing Failure

On March 1, 2001, two modest financial institutions—The Business Bank (TBB) and Keynes Rational—merged to form Capitec Bank. With the merger, Capitec obtained its much-coveted banking licence. The name, derived from the fusion of "capital" and "technology," was aspirational and reflected the bankers' ambitions to ensure ample capital and technology to drive their operations. Werner Du Plessis came up with the name "Capitech." Carl Fisher crossed out the "h".

At the outset, they had a micro-loan book, limited capital, and no technology to offer banking services. PSG Investment Bank Holdings injected R58 million, a lifeline to help Capitec weather its infancy. However, survival would take far more capital in a turbulent sector and economy.

By August 2001, Capitec's numbers told a surprising and sobering tale. With a loan book of just R72 million, it still managed to generate a pre-tax profit of R35 million. The high profit-to-loan-book ratio was largely due to the fact that loans were typically held for short periods, such as a month or two, allowing Capitec to turn the book over several times a year. For a company with 200 branches and 1,200 employees, the profitability came from fees and interest rates that would have been unthinkably high in mainstream banking. The initial growth came largely from acquisitions of other microlenders whose books relied on payroll-deducted lending to civil servants.

Le Roux understood the business's dependence on the South African worker's salary — and the danger that dependence created. Civil servants often had multiple loans deducted directly from their pay before the money reached their bank accounts. Funeral policies and insurance premiums compounded the strain, leaving many government employees with barely enough to live on. The system was a ticking time bomb primed to explode under any shock.

In July 2000, the Gauteng provincial government banned creditors from collecting loan repayments directly through its payroll system, Persal. The national government followed, and the fallout was immediate. Fortunately, Le Roux had sold Anchor Finance to Unifer at just the right moment, sidestepping the disaster. However, the collapse was catastrophic for others in the sector. Unifer (now owned by ABSA), Saambou, and other microlenders, heavily reliant on Persal deductions, saw their share prices plummet.

It wasn't enough that you couldn't deduct your loan repayments directly from your payrolls. Still, new regulations also outlawed using personal bank cards and PINs for debt collection practices that many microlenders, including the Smartfin branded cash stores, had long relied upon.

Unifer, once a giant in microlending, revealed its house of cards in early 2002. Initially, it admitted to overstating its profits by R20 million, a seemingly minor scandal. But by January, the scale of its problems became clear: non-performing loan provisions had to increase by a staggering R1.78 billion. Unifer had grown its loan book from R3.4 billion to R5.6 billion in the six months to the end of September 2001. When Unifer's parent company, ABSA, revealed the misrepresentation, the impact was brutal, wiping R1 billion off its capital base.

The contagion spread quickly. Saambou, another major player, saw R861 million in retail deposits vanish in three days in January 2002. Saambou's share price fell. Depositors got nervous and queued to withdraw their money from the bank. On February 6, 2002, the share price declined by as much as 46% intraday, sparking a vicious cycle of withdrawals and liquidity crises. By February 9, 2002, Saambou was in curatorship, its operations effectively frozen. In the weeks that followed, the sector experienced a period of upheaval. Smaller banks failed, and even larger ones like BoE struggled with liquidity.

The irony is that Saambou was the darling of the market. Over the seven financial years from 1995 to 2001, earnings grew at an average annual rate of 42%. The personal loans book showed advances increased by 87 per cent just before the collapse. It has been argued in subsequent commentary that political reasons influenced the South African Treasury's decision to allow Saambou, another historically Afrikaner bank, to fail. The Registrar of Banks at the time, also named Christo Wiese — no relation to the businessman — was publicly vocal about his disagreement with Trevor Manuel's decision. He retired shortly thereafter. The curator's subsequent investigation found that Saambou's reported financial position had been misrepresented in the period leading up to the collapse arguably with the purpose of maintaining investor confidence and attempting to halt further fall in the share price.

Between 2000 and 2003, 23 of the 47 registered banks exited the South African system. The same period produced the global Enron and WorldCom collapses — accounting frauds whose central mechanism was executive manipulation of financial statements to support share prices.

Capitec prepared for its debut on the Johannesburg Stock Exchange in the shadow of this crisis—the listing date was 18th February 2002. The timing was, to put it mildly, disastrous. Investors were fleeing anything resembling microlending. Many microlenders operated without proper oversight, offering loans with exorbitant interest rates—sometimes as much as thirty per cent per month—to individuals who were already financially vulnerable. Microlending in South Africa targeted low-income individuals, who were often desperate for credit to meet basic needs. Instead of empowering them economically, many microlenders exploited this desperation for profit. Borrowers were frequently not fully informed about the terms and conditions of the loans, including hidden administrative fees, insurance, and penalties.

The whispered valuation of Capitec Bank Holdings Limited was north of 500 cents per share. On the day of listing, PSG Investment Bank would hold 73% of Capitec Bank Holdings. The plan was that a week after listing, it would unbundle—or distribute—Capitec Bank Holding shares to its shareholders. The biggest of which was the PSG Group. Although the initial expectation was that the share would trade above 500 cents, as long as it was above 275 cents, PSG Investment Bank would record a gain in retained earnings from the unbundling, as the price was higher than its original cost. The higher the share price, the higher the profit they could record. An unbundling above 275 cents per share would also benefit the PSG Group, as PSG Investment Bank was a subsidiary, and its gains would be rolled into group earnings.

PSG Corporate Services attempted to stabilise the opening price above 275 cents, but the market did not cooperate. Capitec's stock plunged to a low of 75 cents and closed at 80 cents on its first day. Price stabilisation by a sponsor on listing is a recognised market practice, distinct from manipulation; in volatile conditions with sellers outnumbering buyers, the practical effect is limited regardless.

For Le Roux's team, the listing failure was a measure of how thoroughly the market had turned against microlending. Even Le Roux's purchase of 1.1 million shares in the open market did not arrest the decline. The association with PSG provided some legitimacy but it was both a boon and a burden, it tied PSG to a sector in freefall. In 2002, with a collapsing share price and a sceptical public, the future was anything but certain.

The February financial year-end loomed, and Capitec's numbers looked grim. Headline earnings were flat, and the issuance of additional shares during the listing diluted earnings per share. The market, already punishing PSG for its exposure to microlending, would undoubtedly react harshly. Until 2000, the PSG Group's share price had always traded at a premium to its net asset value (NAV). The group managed to compound its growth in NAV by 75% from 1995 to 2002, whereas its share price only compounded at 34%.

The market rated PSG Group poorly because of its significant exposure to Capitec, a microlending business, and PSG Investment Bank, a third-tier bank. The listing, intended to be a milestone of success, became a desperate gambit.

The market punished PSG for its exposure to Capitec and to PSG Investment Bank, a third-tier bank. PSG's share price, which had been R19 in 1999, was now R4.80 — trading at roughly a 54% discount to NAV. The listing, intended as a milestone, had become a crisis.

Jannie Mouton and his PSG team had the impossible task of driving the Capitec Bank share price above 275 cents before Capitec shares would be unbundled from PSG Investment Bank. They desperately attempted to support the share price the entire week. On Friday, February 22nd, PSG Corporate Services purchased shares, and Le Roux and Stassen bought shares at around 150 cents, but the Capitec share price wouldn't hold, and it closed for the weekend at just 113 cents.

On Monday, the 25th of February, PSG Group ended up with approximately 52% of the share capital of Capitec Bank Holdings. PSG Investment Bank recognised a significant loss from the unbundling — a bitter blow ahead of the February financial year-end for it and its parent company. The numbers didn't just sting—this little unloved microlender was endangering all Jannie Mouton had built up in the PSG Group. He wanted nothing more to do with this micro-lender.

Another danger was that the PSG Group was trading at a significant discount to its underlying assets, making it ripe for a hostile takeover attempt. ABSA, a banking giant, had circled PSG like a predator, hoping to pick apart its discounted assets and retain the crown jewels: PSG Investment Bank.

With time short, Mouton turned to Stellenbosch. Markus Jooste, then rising in the corporate world, and his partner Bruno Steinhoff began acquiring PSG Group stock, helping to defend it against the potential takeover. The brotherhood was operating exactly as the unwritten rules said it would, and just in time. On the day Capitec unbundled from PSG Investment Bank, Mouton picked up the phone.

14. Ethical Failure

To the 12 months ended February 2003:

Start Price	Close Price	% Inc.	Market-Cap	Dividends Decl.	NAV / Share
117c	**260c**	**122%**	**R164m**	**19c**	**607c**

The damage from the listing was done. What Mouton needed now was not just capital but someone who could see a path through and who had gained some public respect. He approached Jooste and invited him onto the PSG Group board. Jooste accepted.

The mechanism Jooste proposed was a last-minute transaction involving selling Key Distributors to PSG Corporate Services. It would later be seen as characteristic of his approach: technically defensible under the accounting standards of the time, but structured in a way that produced the desired earnings outcome rather than reflecting the underlying economics of the business.

Time was short. Le Roux was carrying a vision that the market had not yet validated; Mouton was running the financial calculations. Both were under pressure.

By mid-March 2002, Capitec was again a penny stock, trading at 80 cents. For Mouton, this wasn't just bad optics; it was existential. Capitec had already guided the market on earnings, but the market did not appreciate the trading update. Mouton wanted to eliminate PSG Investment Bank and Capitec Bank Holdings from PSG Group—but not at 80 cents a share. Jooste, ever the pragmatist, approached André Benjamin La Grange and offered a reprieve through some financial alchemy. Le Roux was reportedly not a party to the discussions that took place behind closed doors, but he would have had to approve the financial transactions.

According to accounts later reconstructed from the audit memoranda and the subsequent SENS disclosures, Jooste's argument to La Grange was direct: the guided numbers would not move the share price, and the 2003 forecast was worse. The proposed mechanism used an assessed loss Capitec had inherited from The Business Bank acquisition — selling an asset at a profit before financial year-end, and unwinding the deal before the tax consequences crystallised.

The "something" was Key Distributors, a small, largely dormant Capitec subsidiary established to handle fast-moving consumer goods for informal markets. The solution was ingenious: PSG Corporate Services would "buy" the business for R3.5 million more than recorded on the books on the last day of the financial year, boosting Capitec's earnings by the same amount.[62] A day later, Capitec would repurchase most of it - in this case, 75%. On paper, the manoeuvre worked like a charm.

"You never have to transfer cash," Jooste said, or at least words to that effect. "It's just numbers on a page; journal entries; the auditors would sign off provided the disclosure was made."

---

[62] See SENS published on 4 April 2002. Accessed at: https://sharedata.co.za/v2/Scripts/SENS.aspx?id=33692 Accessed on: 19 December 2024.

PwC was not enthusiastic. The audit head drafted a two-page Significant Matters Memorandum (SMM) flagging the transaction. The memorandum flagged the transaction as related-party, requiring disclosure to avoid the appearance of manipulation.

PwC permitted the disclosure but the memorandum recorded their concern. Auditor standards required them to identify material misstatements, not to prevent disclosed but ethically questionable transactions; this distinction matters throughout what follows.

Jooste and La Grange convinced Mouton that their actions were acceptable corporate conduct. As the majority shareholder, Mouton may have had undue influence over the board at the time, so it would be unfair to speculate that all Capitec directors were in favour of the plan. André Du Plessis had joined the Capitec board, but he was not yet the Financial Director. Du Plessis' appointment was announced on SENS a day after these results came out.[63]

When Capitec published its maiden results on 4 April 2002, it stunned the market. Instead of stagnant growth, as it had guided, the bank reported R48 million in headline earnings, up from the forecasted R45.4 million. Headline earnings per share were 80,2 cents. The share price immediately soared 62% from 90 to 146 cents within hours. It was still trading at less than twice its earnings. Mouton pounced at the opportunity to snap up 170,000 shares. For a brief, heady moment, Capitec's survival seemed possible.

Capitec repurchased 75% of Key Distributors the next day, 1 March 2002. The auditors flagged the transaction in the following year's accounts. The profit warranties on the original sale were not met —

[63] See SENS dated 5 April 2002. Accessed at: https://sharedata.co.za/v2/Scripts/SENS.aspx?id=33721 Accessed on 19 December 2024.

predictably — which allowed the directors to reverse the transaction's effects by 2005, netting out the original R3.5 million.

Over the first 22 years that Capitec has been listed and reported its results, it has consistently obtained PwC audited results, with a full annual report issued within a month of the financial year-end. In 2024, PwC[64] completed its last audit of Capitec, having served as the primary auditors from 2002 to 2024. A mandatory audit firm rotation policy to enhance auditor independence becomes effective for Capitec in the 2025 financial year, with Deloitte and KPMG acting as joint auditors. It is worth noting that the Capitec cell-captives have their auditors, and BDO audits AvaFin. We'll come back to why this is important later.

The bank's antics were about survival, crafted from a small measure of audacity. La Grange and Jooste's gambit added R37 million to Capitec's market cap in a single day, a lifeline for a company then worth less than R100 million.

None of those involved could have foreseen how Jooste would, years later, work with André La Grange's son — Ben La Grange, Steinhoff's CFO — in what would become one of the largest accounting frauds in South African history. La Grange's specific role at Steinhoff has been the subject of regulatory findings, JSE settlements, and his own subsequent admissions; the broader picture, as established by the PwC investigation, was that the misstatement of Steinhoff's financials required cooperation at the senior financial level.

Looking back across many years, it is difficult to know whether Le Roux and du Plessis attempted to stop these first-year manoeuvres

[64] PricewaterhouseCoopers

or accepted them as the price of survival. The most generous reading — and one consistent with what they later built — is that they were largely passive bystanders.

15. Capital Punishment

To the 12 months ended February 2004:

Start Price	Close Price	% Inc.	Market-Cap	Dividends Decl.	NAV / Share
260c	**580c**	**123%**	**R399m**	**20c**	**619c**

PSG could support a share price for a few days. It could not, and would not, refinance the entire business. Mouton made this clear to the Capitec board: the bank was running out of capital, and his wallet was not the answer.

Within days of the failed listing, Mouton was already planning to unbundle more of PSG's Capitec holdings. The man wasn't just hedging his bets but packing his parachute.

Capitec's cost-to-income ratio — the standard measure of banking efficiency — stood at 84% in its first year as a listed entity. Most established banks operated at or below 50%. The gap was a warning.

The business model required relentless execution. Every overdue loan triggered a phone call or SMS — the digital equivalent of a polite nudge. No borrower was too small to track. If you owed Capitec money, Capitec was contacting you.

Ever the numbers man, Stassen calculated that running a Capitec branch cost 34% more than operating a microlending branch. Part of that was maintaining a consistent corporate identity — you could not put a handmade sign over the door and call it a bank. Part was the additional regulatory burden. Month by month, Capitec was converting FinAid branches into Capitec-branded outlets, and the bank hired a young manager from Boland Bank, who had been through its own conversion into PEP Bank, to oversee the rollout. His title — National Conversion Manager — captured the job exactly. He was particularly effective at persuading sceptical branch staff that new signage and a new brand would lead to better days.

That man was Faick Davids. He would rise to a senior position at Capitec and, by his own account, was the brain behind the multi-loan product — and behind an automated mechanism for rolling customers' arrears into their existing active loan accounts. When he left for African Bank in 2009, Capitec sued him, alleging the misuse of confidential information and breach of restraint. The litigation became one of the more closely watched intellectual-property cases in South African banking. The product and the mechanism that Davids says he developed at Capitec will become important to a later chapter; for now, it is enough to note that the man who began his career converting branch signage went on to claim authorship of the technical machinery at the centre of Capitec's loan book.

Capitec's gamble wasn't paying off fast enough. By April 2002, Capitec was running on shareholders' capital with no clear path to profitability and insolvency was looming like a dark cloud over a summer picnic. The irony was delicious—a bank that couldn't pay its bills.

The PSG lifeboat was no longer an option. Having warned Le Roux about the impending cash crunch, Mouton was already knee-deep in "Project Unlock"—unbundling Capitec shares to PSG shareholders at a ratio of 33.08 Capitec shares for every 100 PSG shares held.

With no banks willing to lend, Le Roux, Stassen, and du Plessis took out personal loans and stood surety themselves to keep Capitec funded. They were betting their personal balance sheets on the bank's survival. It wasn't just a vote of confidence in the bank but a high-stakes poker game where they all went in with their chips.

Every loan carried roughly R57 in administrative costs against an average loan size of R602. The margins were unworkable at that scale. Capitec needed larger loans to achieve profitability. Du Plessis approached other banks for funding and was politely declined; after Saambou and Unifer, lending to a high-risk microlender was not on offer.

It wasn't until early 2004 that a breakthrough occurred. Du Plessis convinced the United States Agency for International Development (USAID) to provide a guarantee. With that backing, Futuregrowth became the first institution to offer Capitec a R50 million loan over a five-year period. Once one domino fell, others followed suit. The capital problem was finally easing.

The cost-to-income ratio fell steadily: 84% in 2004, 81% in 2005, 73% by year-end 2005, 66% in 2006, 60% by 2007 — bringing Capitec within reach of the established big-four banks on efficiency.

Attracting deposits required credibility. Capitec's Global One account offered 10% interest on balances up to R25,000 — exceptionally generous, and a clear signal to savers that the bank wanted retail money. By early 2026, that rate had dropped to just 2% — a stark reminder that banks are in the business of making money off interest-rate differentials.

To the 12 months ended February 2005:

Start Price	Close Price	% Inc.	Market-Cap	Dividends Decl.	NAV / Share
580c	**1490c**	**157%**	**R1bn**	**30c**	**672c**

Back in 2003, Capitec had no deposits. By the end of the year, it had attracted R25 million, rising to R48 million by the close of 2004. The loan from Futuregrowth helped boost its cash reserves to R160 million. Deposits, however, were still limited—a mere R74 million in 2005. The numbers weren't just tiny; they were a reality check that showed that trust in Capitec wasn't widespread.

Apparently, in 2005, Riaan Stassen wanted the bank to go to the people, so they bought a Toyota Tazz and converted the boot of the car into a consultant station. The Tazz was a secretive project, with only eight people knowing about the "bank in the boot of a car."[65]

But by 2006, things began to shift. Retail deposits surged to R314 million, and the number of savings clients doubled to 375,000. Come 2007, Capitec was thriving, not just surviving. It had crossed the one-million-client milestone, and deposits surged to R554 million. Psychologically, that was a turning point. The bank was no longer a scrappy underdog; it was becoming a serious contender.

With more deposits came more lending. Loan disbursements climbed to R2.86 billion in 2006 and hit R3.45 billion by 2007. But growth, as always, came at a cost. Bad debts rose from 1.45% of repayments in 2005 to over 4% by 2007, a sobering reminder that managing unsecured loans was no walk in the park. Capitec's journey was a balancing act of attracting deposits, lending wisely, and controlling costs.

The bank's share price told its tale of transformation: up 122% in 2003, another 123% in 2004, nearly tripling in 2005, and doubling again by the 2007 financial year to R37. Investors were sitting up and noticing. Even Jannie Mouton, who had once kept his distance, began wondering if it was time for PSG Group to take a bigger bite of the Capitec pie.

[65] Masipa, M (2022), The Rise & Success of Capitec Bank, Entrepreneur Hub SA, Accessed at: https://entrepreneurhubsa.co.za/the-rise-success-of-capitec-bank/ Accessed on: 20 Nov 2024

16. Accounting Standards

To the 12 months ended February 2006:

Start Price	Close Price	% Inc.	Market-Cap	Dividends Decl.	NAV / Share
1490c	**3105c**	**108%**	**R2,2bn**	**78c**	**784c**

Amid the global financial crisis of 2008/09, Capitec managed to keep its metaphorical boat afloat while others were busy bailing water. The story it sold was that its “low-risk lending practices” and “conservative loan policies” acted like an impenetrable life vest, shielding it from the economic tempests that sank other financial titans. Of course, it's always easier to be the hero of your own story when you're the one writing it.

The collapse of Lehman Brothers in 2008 was akin to watching the world's largest Jenga tower come crashing down. Those investigating the cause of the collapse found that Lehman had removed up to $50 billion in liabilities, exploiting an accounting loophole with FAS 140. This loophole allowed specific repos to be treated as asset sales if they were over 105% collateralised. While deceptive, what Lehman was doing was not technically illegal.

Banks are deeply interconnected. When one bank's assets lose value, it spreads distress throughout the global financial system. Between 2008 and 2009, 165 banks reportedly failed in the United States alone.

Capitec's profits continued to grow through 2009. During the same period, debt review applications and sequestrations reached record highs. One suggestion was that Capitec was, increasingly, the bank of last resort for borrowers turned away elsewhere.

Rising impairments — the provisions a bank holds against expected loan losses — would have constrained the reported earnings and, by extension, the share price. Capitec's accounting choices around impairments through this period merit closer examination.

Capitec's CEO Gerrie Fourie has stated publicly, on multiple occasions, that the bank does not focus on the share price. The bank's remuneration structure, with executive incentives tied to share price appreciation, is in some tension with that claim.

Numbers can bend the truth without breaking it. Accounting standards constrain outright fraud but leave significant room for interpretation. New rules typically reward those who learn to operate within them most aggressively.

Banking is a business of perceptions, and a bank's loan book—the sum of all the money it has lent out—acts as a report card. Investors and analysts pore over it to determine whether the bank is thriving or struggling. So, when accounting standards for loans and recoveries started to shift, Capitec's leadership spotted a golden opportunity hidden in the so-called "grey zone". It was an opportunity to dress up the numbers without technically crossing any lines.

By this period, PSG was firmly re-engaged with Capitec, and Jooste sat on PSG's board. There is no evidence of his direct involvement in Capitec's accounting decisions, but the corporate environment around Capitec was one in which aggressive accounting treatment was familiar to the senior figures involved.

The relevant accounting shift was from incurred-loss to expected-credit-loss provisioning under IFRS 9, which became effective globally in 2018. Capitec's treatment of impairments in the years preceding adoption — under IAS 39's incurred-loss model — produced reported figures that an expected-loss framework would have presented differently. The treatment was within the standards then applicable; whether it was within the spirit of conservative banking provisioning is a separate question entirely.

Under the prior treatment, IAS30, Capitec wrote off loans overdue for more than three months and recognised any subsequent recoveries were treated as delightful surprises and would be recognised as new income. Under the revised treatment, the bank could recognise the present value of estimated future recoveries on the balance sheet — increasing the gross loan book and turnover by the estimated recoveries. It's a minor tweak, sure, but one with significant implications.

In 2009, Capitec added R11.3 million to its loan book representing the present value of expected future recoveries — a treatment that increased headline earnings by 5.4%.[66] The treatment was technically permissible under the IFRS 9 accounting standards. Save

[66] Capitec 2009 Annual Financial Statements pg. 20

for the fact, that a more conservative approach would have required also offsetting estimated future credit losses against the recoveries; Capitec's disclosure did not present the offsetting position with equal prominence. While arguably deceptive and beneficial for Capitec's financials, it wasn't illegal. Keep in mind that it wasn't technically illegal for Lehman Brothers to exploit the loophole in FAS 140 either.

By the following year, Capitec doubled-down the magic trick, adding another R15.6 million in impairments to gross loans.[67] Over a two-year period, the bank generated R38 million in future recoveries. Du Plessis had expertly optimised the ratios analysts cared about most, making the numerator smaller and the denominator larger—the financial equivalent of wearing vertical stripes to appear slimmer. Capitec's manoeuvre fell squarely into that "grey zone" where the rules were arguably open to interpretation, but should have required meticulous disclosure and defensible assumptions.

Imagine if you could provide for future sales in your business—report them today, pat yourself on the back for record-breaking revenue, obtain your bonus, but hold off paying tax on those sales until they happen. A bit of accounting magic that probably garnered a round of back-slapping in the boardroom.

Critics might argue that Du Plessis didn't overreach. After all, recoveries in 2009 were R46 million, climbing to R72 million in 2010 and reaching R100 million by 2011. But there's more to that story—

[67] Capitec 2010 Annual Financial Statements pg. 95

something we'll dissect in a future chapter about how the multi-loan product worked and how they calculated recoveries. What's more telling is how Capitec's provisioning trends steadily declined, even as the loan book grew rapidly. On paper, it all looked marvellously optimistic.

Capitec's executives had a polished narrative. They claimed their loan book quality improved thanks to better due diligence and tighter credit controls. Default rates were stabilising, and recoveries were climbing. Yet, how did the bank go from no recoveries in 2007 to R100 million by 2011?

By 2012, the fine print of Capitec's results was beginning to tell a more complicated story than the headline numbers suggested.

17. Arch Equity

To the 12 months ended February 2007:

Start Price	Close Price	% Inc.	Market-Cap	Dividends Decl.	NAV / Share
3105c	**3700c**	**19%**	**R3bn**	**45c**	**1175c**

Capitec's unbundling from PSG Group in December 2003 reduced PSG's holding from 58% to just 15.6%, but Mouton personally retained 331,088 Capitec shares — and what looked like free float was, in practice, within reach of the broader PSG network. Let me explain.

Firstly, we need to understand the context of the South African landscape and remember that Mouton is a master capital allocator who understands what drives equity prices. Some key drivers are GDP and interest rates. Bank share prices tend to perform better when interest rates rise, but South Africa has just entered a falling interest rate cycle. Former Reserve Bank Governor Tito Mboweni cut interest rates by 450 basis points in 2003 and then reduced the repo rate by a further 50 basis points in August 2004 and again in April 2005.

In December 2003, Capitec Bank tentatively entered the choppy waters of Broad-Based Black Economic Empowerment (BEE) with a staff share purchase plan. On the surface, it was a heartfelt attempt to empower employees, as those who received Capitec shares were offered a 10% discount with no transaction costs. It was practically a bazaar without the soggy sausage rolls. Yet, even as 105 employees signed up, it became clear that this modest gesture wouldn't win Capitec any gold stars on the BEE scorecard.

Enter Piet Mouton, son of PSG founder Jannie Mouton. Piet understood that appearances were as vital as substance in the world of BEE. Arch Equity is a private equity firm that Piet initially controlled. But in a politically savvy twist, Desmond Lockey—a golf-playing ANC parliamentarian with a talent for being in the right place at the right time—appeared as a shareholder. It all started with a chance meeting at a golf tournament. In South Africa, politics and finance seem best played on the green.

Arch Equity, now listed on the JSE, began acquiring Capitec shares with the enthusiasm of a child in a candy shop—6% by February 2004, 14% by August, and by the end of 2005, over 20%. Under the watchful eye of the Mouton clan, Arch Equity began quietly acquiring a significant stake in Capitec, sending a clear message: Mouton wasn't letting go of Capitec; he was simply hedging his bets.

Capitec always seemed hesitant to rush to check all its BEE boxes. Capitec's convoluted BEE schemes and curious alliances will show why Black Economic Empowerment is an idea that seemed doomed to failure. Those who give away part of their company do so under duress, utilising structures and agreements that ensure they maintain a modicum of control. Those who obtain their shares do so with more interest in their future payday than in the underlying business. It is a marriage of convenience, with one partner in it for the divorce, where they get their final settlement, sometimes at the cost of innocent employees.

Lockey's presence on the Arch Equity board added a politically pleasing shade of empowerment while the real power stayed in the family, much like a puppet show where only the strings change hands. It was a masterstroke by PSG to reclaim control of its financial offspring.

By 2006, PSG Group was again in the limelight on the JSE. The Sunday Times ranked it number one in terms of shareholders' wealth created over the past decade. PSG's share price had soared from 45 cents to 1230 cents, a compounded growth rate of 61.73%. Ironically, the second-best performer was African Bank, which, as we now know, ultimately proved to be as financially stable as a house of cards in a wind tunnel.

Had you been fortunate (or prophetic) enough to invest R10,000 in PSG Group back on 17 November 1995, when Mouton picked up his stake in the PAG cash shell, you'd have found yourself sitting on a cool R2.9 million by February 2006.[68] That's a jaw-dropping 74% annualised growth. No wonder they dubbed him the "Boere Buffett."

The Reserve Bank overreacted to the downward trend in interest rates, which fueled a boom, with household consumption rising 6.9% in real terms in 2005 and 8.3% in 2006. Mouton knew that the interest rate cycle had to change, which would suit the banking sector. On the way up, Mboweni hiked interest rates by 550 basis points between June 2006 and June 2008, bringing the prime

[68] Includes unbundled Capitec (CPI) shares which would constitute R716,500 of that amount.

overdraft rate up to 15,5%. Household consumption moved into recession by the third quarter of 2008.

Capitec was also starting to catch more attention than a hyperactive toddler on a sugar rush. Mouton's initial hesitation toward Capitec had proved unfounded. It had now transformed into enthusiasm, and he sought to increase PSG's stake to just under 35%, strategically skirting the threshold that would require a mandatory offer to minority shareholders.

By August 2006, PSG decided it was time for a little corporate matchmaking, and they merged with Arch Equity Limited, incorporating its 20% Capitec stake as part of the union. But mergers, like marriages, come with complications. The deal left Capitec without its BEE shareholder, but we will discuss this in the next chapter. In early 2007, Mouton sought to acquire more of Capitec, so PSG offered a share swap to Capitec shareholders: 1.4545 PSG shares for every Capitec share. This move nudged PSG's stake in Capitec up to 34.9%.

Mouton loved a good story. In PSG's 2008 annual report, he highlighted two investors who each took a R400,000 punt on Capitec post-listing. By the time he was writing, their stakes had ballooned to over R15 million, with another R1 million earned in dividends. If ever there was a case for being a contrarian investor, this was it. It wasn't just smart money; it was clairvoyant money.

To the 12 months ended February 2008:

Start Price	Close Price	% Inc.	Market-Cap	Dividends Decl.	NAV / Share
3700c	**3900c**	**5.1%**	**R3,2bn**	**100c**	**1297c**

Towards the end of 2009, PSG Group's holding in Capitec exceeded 35%, and it was required to make a mandatory offer to shareholders, which it did at 1.5767 PSG Group shares for every Capitec share. Remember that PSG held their shares in Capitec through a subsidiary called PSG Financial Services Limited. By 2010, Capitec was running full throttle, but with growth came the need for fresh capital. The bank launched a R1.05 billion rights issue, set at R125 per share, in January 2011, representing 10% of its issued ordinary share capital. Writing a R367 million cheque to maintain PSG's stake was, as Mouton put it, "a no-brainer."[69]

The new funds allowed Capitec to shift its lending book into longer-term, higher-value loans. By August 2009, 72% of its gross loan book stretched beyond 12 months. Six months later, that figure was 78%, and by August 2010, it had climbed to 83%.[70] Capitec executives obtained an appetite for raising capital. In November 2011, Merrill Lynch International assisted with a bookbuild to raise R800 million by placing 4,644,952 new shares at R172 each. Merrill

---

[69] PSG Group 2011 Annual Financial Statement p.5

[70] Ndzamela, P (2010), Capitec gets capital hungry, Moneyweb, Accessed at: https://www.moneyweb.co.za/archive/capitec-gets-capital-hungry/ Accessed on: 20 November 2024.

Lynch then went on to help underwrite another rights issue in October 2012 for 14 million new shares, raising R2.2 billion.

To the 12 months ended February 2009:

Start Price	Close Price	% Inc.	Market-Cap	Dividends Decl.	NAV / Share
3900c	**3001c**	**- 23%**	**R2,5bn**	**140c**	**1512c**

The 2012 rights issue was interesting. Capitec had recently traded as high as R220 a share, but the rights issue was at R160. When the Nil Paid Letters (NPL) were issued, the share price dropped to around R200 each, but this still valued each NPL at around R40. PSG Financial Services could sell NPLs to create capital while not being too concerned about following all their rights. PSG Financial Services sold NPLs, reducing its shareholding in Capitec from 32.2% to 28.5%, but it received its original investment in Capitec back in cash.

18. Dark Sides

To the 12 months ended February 2010:

Start Price	Close Price	% Inc.	Market-Cap	Dividends Decl.	NAV / Share
3001c	**8200c**	**173%**	**R6,8bn**	**210c**	**1896c**

Capitec, long marketed as the champion of the ordinary South African, has had a complicated relationship with Black Economic Empowerment. BEE compliance is required of all large South African corporations, regardless of when they were founded; Capitec was no exception.

Other banks also had their challenges in implementing B-BBEE. ABSA initially brought Tokyo Sexwale on board. Sexwale exited the position at the earliest opportunity available under the lock-in. In 2004, after Barclays acquired a majority stake in ABSA, it created Batho Bonke Capital to facilitate a B-BBEE transaction, thereby giving ordinary black South Africans a 10% stake in the company. In 2005, Nedbank launched its Eyethu Ownership Plan, which allowed more than 500,000 black South Africans, including employees and clients, to take a stake in the bank.

While the Big Four banks routinely achieve Level One BEE ratings, the best Capitec could ever muster was Level Two, occasionally slipping to Level Four until the breakthrough year of 2024.[71] The reasons for this are complex and have a lot to do with reluctance in introducing token black, politically connected shareholders.

If you will recall, Capitec's first foray into BEE was with Desmond Lockey and Arch Equity. He was a non-reluctant seller when PSG wanted the stake back, causing Capitec to lose its BEE rating. To address this, on 12 December 2006, Capitec issued 10 million shares to Coral Lagoon Investments 194 (Pty) Ltd, which was then wholly owned by Ash Brook Investments 15 (Pty) Ltd. Ash Brook was owned by a consortium of 13 black shareholders, notably the spouses of ANC heavyweights Pilisiwe Twala-Tau and Gugu Mtshali. Coral Lagoon secured a 12.2% stake in Capitec for R300 million—courtesy of a R285 million loan from the government-owned Industrial Development Corporation.

However, the deal wasn't without strings. Coral paid R30 per share, a 15% discount to the market price, and agreed to conditions that required Capitec's consent for any future sales, and only to black buyers as defined by the BBBEE Act.

After holding for five years, Coral sold over 5 million shares to the government-owned Public Investment Corporation (PIC) to repay its IDC loan. Capitec's consent was required, and they imposed a further 10-year lock-in period for the remaining shares.

Fast-forward to 2015, and Lebashe Investments came knocking, offering to buy Capitec shares from the PIC at a steep discount.

[71] By August 2009, 72% of its gross loan book stretched beyond 12 months. Six months later, that figure lower compliance.

Lebashe's directors included former PIC bigwigs.[72] Despite criticism, the deal eventually went through, and the PIC even funded the purchase.[73] The Lebashe Investments / PIC transaction structure became the subject of public controversy and was examined in detail during the Mpati Commission of Inquiry into the Public Investment Corporation (2019). The Commission's findings on this and related PIC transactions are part of the public record.

In 2017, Coral attempted to sell more shares to Petratouch (Pty) Ltd, a 100% black-owned company. Capitec approved the sale with conditions. The sale resulted in Coral taking a 52% haircut on the share price—a financial trim they weren't happy about.

By 2019, Regiments Capital, infamous for its connections to the Guptas, owned 60% of Ash Brook, the holding company of Coral Lagoon. Investigations into state capture revealed the Regiments' involvement in dubious financial activities, which resulted in significant losses for state-owned entities, including Transnet. Regiments agreed to transfer R500 million worth of Capitec shares to the Transnet Second Defined Benefit Fund as part of a settlement agreement. But when asked to consent to the sale, Capitec refused.

---

[72] Their directors included Tshepo Mahloele, a former chairman of the Public Investment Corporation (PIC), Jabu Moleketi, a former deputy finance minister of Treasury and executive at the PIC, and Warren Wheatley, also with a controversial past tied to state finances. Conduct your own research into some of these scandals, I suggest you start with the Oilgate Scandal, then Harith and Tiso-Blackstar to start you down the rabbithole. Wheatley was a former director of the FPI an institution with a haze of controversy over how candidates were approved to offer private equity services to the PIC.

[73] A certain Asset Manager provided me with details of Lebashe acquiring some Capitec Bank shares from Marcytouch (Pty) Ltd and Ergold (Pty) when the directors of these companies namely Litha Nohanye and Niven Pillay from Regiments Capital - who were also Capitec BEE partners - were under asset freeze by the National Prosecuting Authority. I wasn't able to confirm the details before finalising the book.

Judge Bashier Vally called them out, noting that Capitec seemed more concerned with its BEE scorecard[74] than ethical restitution and distancing itself from tainted shareholders.[75]

Capitec's response was a masterclass in PR spin, claiming that the sale didn't require their consent. Meanwhile, Coral Lagoon sought legal action to try and recoup the R1,225 billion difference between the market price and the 52% discount on the sale to Petratouch. But all that Coral got from the claim was a bitter aftertaste.

In addition to external BEE shareholders, Capitec has also focused on internal empowerment. In 2022, Capitec launched a fresh BEE scheme, offering shares worth R1 billion to employees at a 50% discount. Capitec-backed loans were issued to staff to cover the purchase, with dividends earmarked for repayment. According to the B-BBEE Certificate for Capitec Bank Holdings Limited for 2024, the company achieved a Level One Contributor status, with an equity ownership score of 23.69.

Beneath the glossy veneer of empowerment lay a more profound truth about South Africa's financial landscape: BEE has often been about political connections and backroom deals rather than genuine economic transformation. The system has primarily benefited a few well-connected elite individuals, leaving the broader goal of uplifting the majority as elusive as a mirage.

---

[74] Bezuidenhout, J (2019), *Regiments Capital puts up R500m in Capitec shares,* Daily Maverick. Accessed at: https://www.dailymaverick.co.za/article/2019-08-27-exclusive-regiments-capital-puts-up-r500m-in-capitec-shares-in-lieu-of-state-capture-claims/ Accessed on: 24 July 2024

[75] Ryan, C (2019), *How The State Capture Project Washed Up on Capitec's Door*, Moneyweb. Accessed at: https://www.moneyweb.co.za/news/companies-and-deals/how-the-state-capture-project-washed-up-on-capitecs-door/ Accessed on: 24 November 2024

19. Striking Growth

To the 12 months ended February 2011:

Start Price	Close Price	% Inc.	Market-Cap	Dividends Decl.	NAV / Share
8200c	**15901c**	**94%**	**R14,9bn**	**290c**	**3418c**

South Africa's inequality is among the most extreme in the world. The country's Gini coefficient, around 0.63 [2020], reflects a deep divide rooted in the racial and economic structures of the apartheid era and the slow pace of transformation since.[76]

The Big Four — FirstRand, ABSA, Standard, and Nedbank — were highly profitable but structurally unable to compete with Capitec on price. They had little appetite for clients whose accounts would not generate fee income beyond the basics. Capitec's smaller, simpler structure let it move faster on product and pricing than the larger banks could.

The country needed broader financial inclusion. Mobile banking was in its infancy, internet access was largely desktop-bound, and most low-income transactions happened in cash. How to bank the unbanked was an open question.

In 2004, the Financial Sector Charter launched the Mzansi savings account, a low-cost banking solution for underserved South Africans. Backed by major banks and Postbank, it promised easy access with

[76] University of Cape Town, Accessed at: www.news.uct.ac.za/article/-2021-05-21-inequality-in-south-africa-is-a-ticking-timebomb Accessed on: 20 November 2024

minimal documentation, shared infrastructure, and a single ATM withdrawal fee across networks. By 2008, over six million accounts had been opened, primarily by black South Africans, but the results fell short. Many accounts saw minimal use or immediate withdrawals, undermining the initiative's viability. By the mid-2010s, all South African banks replaced their Mzansi accounts with new products.

Capitec, a signatory to the Charter, skipped Mzansi and went directly to the same market, undercutting competitors with cheaper offerings. By 2010, with 2.5 million clients drawn largely from the unbanked or underbanked, Capitec was becoming systemically important — not in the sense of being too large to fail, but in the sense of being too necessary to fail. Regulators and policymakers now had an interest in its continued success. The Mzansi initiative's failure had shown what happened when transactional banking for the low-income segment was attempted by committee. Capitec had succeeded where the consortium had not, and that success now carried weight.

Between 2008 and 2012, Capitec's gross loans and advances rose from R2 billion to R18.4 billion, climbing to R24.7 billion six months later. The growth was extraordinary. Capitec's competitor in unsecured lending, African Bank, was on the same trajectory, but African Bank's parallel growth would end very differently.

In August 2012, the police shooting of 34 striking miners at Marikana became South Africa's defining post-apartheid labour tragedy. The deeper context included unsecured lending. It did not cause the massacre, but it shaped the wage pressure that drove the strike.

To the 12 months ended February 2012:

Start Price	Close Price	% Inc.	Market-Cap	Dividends Decl.	NAV / Share
15901c	**18500c**	**16.3%**	**R18,5bn**	**425c**	**4962c**

The striking miners were not just demanding higher wages from Lonmin; many were carrying loans whose servicing costs left little of their take-home pay. Microlenders, including the major unsecured lenders, were active in the mining communities. Workers' indebtedness was an unstated but significant factor in the wage demands.

Pravin Gordhan, then Minister of Finance, moved to tighten regulations on unsecured lending. Among the practices under scrutiny was the widespread use of emolument attachment orders — court-mandated deductions from wages, commonly called garnishee orders.

The abuses were well-documented. Lenders held borrowers' ID cards as informal security, charged interest at rates close to the legal cap, and routinely obtained EAOs in magistrates' courts far from where borrowers lived — effectively eliminating the borrower's opportunity to contest the order. The University of Stellenbosch Legal Aid Clinic would, in 2015, take this practice to the Constitutional Court. The matter was decided on 13 September 2016.

One detail worth noting about the Stellenbosch Legal Aid Clinic's role in the EAO litigation is that Capitec has, over a number of years, been a significant funder of the University of Stellenbosch Law Faculty[77]— of which the Clinic is part. The Clinic itself maintained, and the university confirmed, that funding from any donor did not direct the Clinic's case selection. The Constitutional Court judgment in 2016[78] named several lenders whose EAO practices had generated the litigation; Capitec was not among the principal targets. The case primarily concerned smaller and more aggressive lenders whose abuses were both more visible and harder to defend. The result was a reform that constrained the worst practices in the sector while leaving Capitec's collections model broadly intact.

A cynic might find the alignment of interests too neat: a major funder of the Law Faculty whose own collections practices were broadly insulated from a reform that constrained its smaller competitors. A more generous reading is that Capitec, like several other large lenders, had little operational need to defend EAO abuses and substantial reputational interest in seeing them reformed. However, other legal action against Capitec, which we shall consider in a moment, seems to contradict this.

---

[77] Capitec Bank Holdings Limited, Integrated Annual Report's, available at https://www.capitecbank.co.za/investor-relations, noting Capitec's reported social investment in tertiary education including support for the University of Stellenbosch and University of Stellenbosch, Faculty of Law, donor acknowledgements, available at the Faculty's published materials or annual report.

[78] University of Stellenbosch Legal Aid Clinic and Others v Minister of Justice and Correctional Services and Others [2016] ZACC 32; 2016 (6) SA 596 (CC); 2016 (12) BCLR 1535 (CC). Judgment delivered 13 September 2016.

Despite Gordhan's proposed reforms, including outlawing EAOs for loans, the structural drivers of South African indebtedness — low wages, high unemployment, limited access to formal credit at reasonable rates — were beyond the reach of consumer credit regulation.

To the 12 months ended February 2013:

Start Price	Close Price	% Inc.	Market-Cap	Dividends Decl.	NAV / Share
18500c	**18800c**	**1.6%**	**R21,5bn**	**574c**	**7212c**

Capitec's rapid growth in unsecured lending mirrored the fragility of the broader economy. South African GDP growth averaged 2% annually between 2011 and 2014, constrained by labour unrest, scheduled power cuts known locally as load-shedding, and weak global demand. The Zuma presidency added political uncertainty and the corruption that would later be documented as state capture.

In January 2013, Amplats[79] announced plans to suspend operations at two Rustenburg mines and retrench up to 14,000 workers. The timing couldn't have been worse. Workers were already negotiating for a minimum monthly wage, the issue that sparked the Lonmin strikes. The ANC and mining unions[80] were outraged by Amplats' announcement. After heated consultations, the mines reduced the retrenchment figure to 6,000 workers—but this didn't placate the unions. They gave management until 17 May 2013 to agree to the

[79] Anglo American Platinum, a South African based miner
[80] COSATU, NUM and AMCU.

wage demands—or face more strikes.[81] And strike they did, for months on end.

Court papers would later reveal a sobering statistic: during the Amplats strike, roughly 10,500 employees took out an average of nearly 15 loans each, with every loan carrying a 12% initiation fee. It was a veritable debt spiral. The Plaintiff, Summit Financial Services, argued that this was reckless lending as defined under the National Credit Act.

These years of practising the sin of reckless lending would return to haunt Capitec in June 2024, but only briefly. Several successful applications have been made through the Courts to rescind fraudulent garnishee orders. Successful claims for the repayment of all debt, fees and interest accompanied some of these.

For Capitec, these years were paradoxical. On one hand, the bank's loan book expanded, its market share grew, and its profitability remained robust. On the other hand, the risks became impossible to ignore. By 2014, loans past due had risen to 6.5% of gross advances, up from 5.1% just two years prior. Critics warned of a looming credit bubble in South Africa's unsecured lending market—a bubble that could burst if consumers became over-leveraged.

Capitec's leadership brushed aside these concerns. They pointed to their affordability metrics, highlighting their ability to recover previously written-off loans.

---

[81] De Waal, M (2013), Anglo Platinum strike still looms, Daily Maverick. Accessed at: https://www.dailymaverick.co.za/article/2013-05-17-anglo-platinum-strike-still-looms/ Accessed on: 18 November 2024

To the 12 months ended February 2014:

Start Price	Close Price	% Inc.	Market-Cap	Dividends Decl.	NAV / Share
18800c	**18375c**	**-1.7%**	**R21,2bn**	**663c**	**8433c**

As regulators clamped down on garnishee orders and rogue lending practices, the deeper fault lines of economic inequality remained. In fact, in 2016, the Constitutional Court ruled that the routine practice of allowing magistrates' court clerks to issue garnishee orders, often without the debtor being present, was unconstitutional.

Banks like African Bank and Capitec relied on garnishee orders to collect from debtors who had fallen behind. Where a borrower was employed, an EAO effectively guaranteed payment ahead of other deductions — leaving the borrower with whatever remained, but assuring the lender. The structural effect was to make default risk low at the lender's level and very high at the household level.

Unsecured lending didn't cause the Marikana massacre, but it certainly illuminated the fragility of a system built on borrowed time and borrowed money.

20. Moral Licensing

To the 12 months ended February 2015:

Start Price	Close Price	% Inc.	Market-Cap	Dividends Decl.	NAV / Share
18375c	**41000c**	**123%**	**R47,4bn**	**836c**	**9822c**

Picture a striking miner — let's call him Moses — standing under the blazing sun, shirt damp with sweat and dust from another unrelenting day of striking. His family needed food, and the landlord wouldn't wait forever. Capitec's ATM glinted invitingly across the street. Moses sighed and crossed the road. He needed a loan, just enough to tide him over. He wasn't the only one. The queue wound around the block, each person with their own story and desperation.

Institutions that have built reputations for doing good often receive a pass for behaviour that, in less celebrated organisations, would be questioned. Social psychology calls this "moral licensing." Capitec's reputation for serving the underbanked has provided exactly this licence: the apparent good deed of granting credit to those whom other banks would refuse has functioned as cover for administration fees and interest rates that, in other contexts, would be called exploitative.

Central to this meteoric growth was the moral licensing of a multi-loan product, which blurred the line between innovation and entrapment. Unlike traditional loans, the multi-loan option offered flexibility to clients, allowing them to pre-qualify for a maximum credit limit and draw funds as needed. But every drawdown was treated as a new loan, with its initiation fees and administrative costs.

The mechanics, illustrated through a hypothetical borrower: Moses takes out an initial two-month loan of R5,000 at the start of the financial year, having been pre-approved for a multi-loan facility of up to R50,000.[82] Two months later he returned for R15,000 over six months. Of that R15,000, his unpaid R5,000 is repaid out of the new loan, a fresh initiation fee is deducted, and R8,950 is made available for withdrawal. From Capitec's perspective, the books now show a R5,000 recovery on the previous loan and a R15,000 new loan written. The increase in reported lending and recoveries is R21,050;[83] yet only R8,950 cash was at risk.

Across the full year, the cycle would produce R50,000 in reported recoveries and R95,000 in new loans written, with R3,150 in initiation fees collected. The income statement reflects R148,150 of activity; the maximum cash at risk to the bank at any point is R28,950.[84] Even if Moses defaulted on the full amount, the bank would still show an impressive profit—financial alchemy.

For clients caught in the cycle, the multi-loan worked like a credit ouroboros — each new advance feeding the old, the principal

[82] Capitec described its offer as being a single loan with a term of anywhere between one and 84 months and a maximum amount of R230 000. Clients could choose their own credit plan based on their profile and affordability, and what they required - instead of being bound by predetermined loan terms.

[83] R5k in recoveries, R15k in new sales and R1,050 in initiation fees++

[84] R50k-{R30k-(R8,950+R1,050)+R1,050}=R28,950

growing alongside the fees. Monthly repayments looked manageable in isolation; the underlying debt continued to grow.

Once the mechanism is understood, the rising recoveries pattern in Capitec's financial statements is no longer mysterious. Recoveries rose from R0 in 2007 to R100 million in 2011 to R176 million in 2012, R434 million in 2014, and R1.1 billion by 2017. Capitec attributed the growth to improved debt collection. The mechanism described above provides a more straightforward explanation.

For everything to work according to plan, there was a reliance on the average loan size getting larger. By 2014, the multi-loan's impact was impossible to ignore. The average loan size had surged by 70% year-on-year,[85] driven by longer-term loans that now made up 80% of Capitec's lending. Leadership championed the product as a flexible tool for managing credit needs, but critics saw it differently. The multi-loan was a lead weight pulling clients deeper into debt.

Moses knew none of this as he stared at the ATM screen for the fourth time in a year. The strike was still dragging on; his children were hungry, and the ATM had offered a solution the three previous times he arrived. Capitec's model thrived on this cycle of necessity, each transaction boosting its bottom line while leaving clients like Moses trapped in an unending debt spiral. The only paper he left at the ATM this time read: 'Insufficient Funds.'

By 2017, around two-thirds of Capitec's loan book consisted of first-time borrowers, as new clients continued to join its ranks.

---

[85] In 2003, the average loan size was just R602; by 2007, this had doubled to R1,180; by 2012 it was more than R6,5k

Beneath the success lay an unsettling question: could a bank built on unsecured lending thrive in a country riddled with inequality? So far, the answer appears to be in the affirmative, but as we shall soon see, it does make some sceptical.

The ATM was a gateway to survival and a symbol of entrapment. Capitec's growth in this period was built on borrowers for whom the next loan was always necessary.

Legislation and corporations are ideas that come from privileged intellectuals, and there is a bias that laws tend to favour those with money and know-how over the poor and uneducated. It stands to reason that Capitec will go on to surround itself with an army of attorneys whose sole purpose is to extract what they can from the bank's debtors. This strategy is reflected in Capitec's growing recoveries over the years.

There is something deeply uncomfortable about a courtroom in which a banking institution argues, against a single mother or an indigent borrower, that it holds a moral as well as a legal right to recover its loan in full — when the underlying reason for non-payment is the unforeseen circumstance against which no household at that income level can insure.

21. Predatory Practices

To the 12 months ended February 2016:

Start Price	Close Price	% Inc.	Market-Cap	Dividends Decl.	NAV / Share
41000c	**47400c**	**15.6%**	**R54,8bn**	**1055c**	**11663c**

On 4 May 2016, Summit Financial Partners filed an action against Capitec Bank in the Stellenbosch Magistrate's Court. The complaint focused on the multi-loan product and alleged reckless lending in violation of the National Credit Act. The case attracted attention beyond its immediate parties, because it tested the legal boundary between innovative consumer credit and reckless extension of debt.

At the centre of the dispute was Capitec's multi-loan, a financial Swiss army knife offering customers multiple short-term loans at lightning speed. Convenient? Perhaps. But according to Summit, it came with a catch. They argued that the National Credit Act (NCA) required affordability checks for every loan issued. Yet Capitec treated each withdrawal under the product as a standalone loan, with a fresh initiation fee every time. To Summit, this wasn't innovation but exploitation, dressed in the sharp suit of legal grey areas.

Capitec remained as unflappable as a duck gliding on a pond —never mind the furious paddling beneath the surface. The bank's executives issued a firm denial. "The loan is a one-month facility," they claimed, dismissing the allegations as a mere technicality. They doubled down on their stance that their practices adhered to the NCA. But beneath the calm exterior, the bank's aggressive lending model was under increasing scrutiny, with the multi-loan at its heart. Was it a financial lifeline for cash-strapped clients, as Capitec claimed? Or, as Summit contended, a legal sleight of hand that turned manageable credit into a treadmill of unending debt?[86]

Summit argued that the cumulative effect of multiple initiation fees pushed the total cost of credit for some borrowers to as much as 500% on an annualised basis. Capitec discontinued the multi-loan in November 2015 — but, in Summit's view, replaced it with a similar product under a different name. Summit pursued the matter.

Summit had pursued similar claims against the furniture retailer Lewis in the preceding year. The Capitec case was part of a broader effort to test the limits of permissible lending practice in the unsecured market.

The stakes were significant. Capitec's growth had been built on unsecured lending. A finding of reckless lending in respect of the multi-loan would have implications well beyond the specific matter, both for Capitec and for the sector.

The matter ended not in judgment but in settlement. Capitec and Summit reached an out-of-court agreement, the terms of which were confidential. The settlement made the broader question moot:

---

[86] Wood, J.A. (2016) , JustMoney, *Capitec Bank fails to put the customer first – Summit* Accessed at: https://www.justmoney.co.za/articles/ capitec-bank-fails-to-put-the-customer-first-summit/ Accessed on: 20 November 2024.

no court ruled on whether the multi-loan crossed the line from credit innovation into reckless lending. The context surrounding Summit is worth noting. Summit Financial Partners was, at the time, owned by RMB Holdings — part of the FirstRand group, and therefore a competitor to Capitec. Some commentary at the time suggested that Summit's case was weaker than its rhetoric, and that the litigation reflected competitive rather than purely consumer-protection motives. Capitec's settlement, on its own terms, prevented a judicial finding either way.

Banks must lend. Credit creation is essential to a growing economy, and lending is an accounting transaction that creates money rather than redistributing it from savers to borrowers — a point insufficiently understood in popular discussion. With that creative power comes responsibility. Capitec's non-performing loans rose through this period, but so did its recoveries: by 2017, recoveries reached R1.125 billion, boosting earnings and supporting the share price.

22. Short Wirecard

To the 12 months ended February 2017:

Start Price	Close Price	% Inc.	Market-Cap	Dividends Decl.	NAV / Share
47400c	**72500c**	**53%**	**R83,8bn**	**1250c**	**13809c**

The activist short-seller is a relatively new figure in finance. Activist long investors have existed for a century — buying undervalued companies and pushing management to unlock value. It is generally noted that long investors publish their top holdings and often appear in the media to talk up their book. The short-seller's role is more controversial: build a position against a company you believe to be misrepresenting itself, publish your research, and let the market correct based on the information that you have uncovered.

The activist short trade is asymmetric. If the research is right, the share price falls and the position pays off. If the research is wrong, the position is uncapped on the downside — there is no limit to how high a share price can rise. The short-seller therefore has every incentive to be right, and to be public. This necessity to be public should not be downplayed, because anonymous shorts cannot move the price as decisively as a published thesis. The model rewards thoroughness, exposure, and nerve.

The model also produces casualties. Short-sellers operate against the prevailing direction of every other actor in the market — companies, analysts, asset managers, regulators, media — all of whom have reasons and often incentives to prefer the upward narrative. Being early on a short call is functionally indistinguishable from being wrong. The history of short traders and hedge funds who trade in short positions is littered with casualties of those who saw the fraud, seized the position, and ran out of capital before the fraud was finally admitted or properly exposed.

Fraser Perring, a blunt-spoken, rough-hewn, balding farmer from rural England, did not look like a man who would change German financial regulation. Born on a pig farm in Cornwall, Perring did not take the conventional London route into finance. He studied psychology, trained and worked as a social worker, and came to short-selling sideways, by way of personal interest in corporate misrepresentation. He has no formal qualification in financial services. His detractors have made much of this. His admirers point out that it has not appeared to hold him back.

Perring's approach to research draws on instincts honed in a profession that requires reading people for a living. Social workers spend their careers separating what they are told from what is actually happening, and Perring brings the same instinct to corporate disclosures. He treats financial statements the way he was once trained to treat case files: as documents whose function is to present a version of events, which may or may not correspond to the underlying reality. The job is to find the gap.

This was the approach that, in early 2016, would lead him to Wirecard. What followed would change Perring's life, establish his reputation, and provide the template for everything that came afterwards — including, two years later, his report on Capitec.

In February 2016, Wirecard AG was one of the most celebrated companies in Germany. Listed on the Frankfurt Stock Exchange, included in the DAX, lauded as a homegrown technology champion in a country whose corporate culture had produced relatively few of them, Wirecard had a market capitalisation of roughly €5 billion and was growing rapidly. The company described itself as a payments processor — a digital plumbing business that handled transactions between merchants and consumers, taking a small cut of each.

On 24 February 2016, Fraser Perring and a co-author, Matthew Earl, published the first Zatarra Research report on Wirecard. The report — Zatarra was the pseudonymous research outfit Perring and Earl were operating under — alleged that Wirecard's reported financial performance was inconsistent with the underlying business, that the company had links to money laundering, and that significant portions of its reported revenue could not be substantiated. The report ran to roughly a hundred pages and was densely sourced.

The response was, in retrospect, extraordinary.

Wirecard denied everything. The company described the report as "utterly false" and threatened legal action. BaFin, the German financial regulator, did not investigate Wirecard. Instead, it investigated the short-sellers. BaFin's officials publicly suggested that the Zatarra report was market manipulation; they referred matters to prosecutors; they imposed a temporary ban on new short positions in Wirecard, an almost unprecedented step in a major European market. The German financial press, with rare exceptions, all seemed to side with Wirecard. Wirecard's auditors, EY, continued to sign off on the financials. The share price continued to rise.

Perring and Earl were doxxed. Their identities were revealed and circulated online. They received threats. Earl, who had been short Wirecard since November 2015 and for whom the position had become professionally and personally consuming, eventually withdrew from active short-selling. He has said publicly that the cost was greater than he had been prepared for.

Perring continued. He has since described the years between 2016 and 2020 as the worst of his life. He was the subject of personal attacks in German media. He was the subject of physical surveillance by private investigators hired, it would later emerge, by Wirecard itself. He has spoken publicly about an incident in which he was kidnapped, held against his will and had his life threatened — an episode whose precise details remain disputed but which Perring describes as having been intended to intimidate him into silence.

Perring's thesis was substantially correct, but it would take several years before what he uncovered would be recognised.

In January 2019, the Financial Times's Dan McCrum and his colleagues began publishing what would become a sustained investigation into Wirecard's Asian operations. The FT's reporting, drawing on whistleblowers from inside the company, documented patterns consistent with what Zatarra had alleged three years earlier. True to form, BaFin responded by investigating the FT journalists for market manipulation. The German financial establishment continued to defend their darling listing on the DAX, Wirecard.

In April 2020, KPMG — ostensibly hired by Wirecard to conduct a special investigation intended to rebut the FT — reported that it could not verify the existence of roughly €1 billion of Wirecard's reported cash balances. In June 2020, EY refused to sign off on Wirecard's accounts, citing the same issue. The cash, it transpired, did not exist. It had never existed. Wirecard filed for insolvency on 25 June 2020, with €1.9 billion of reported cash unaccounted for and the CEO, Markus Braun, in custody facing fraud charges. The Chief Operating Officer, Jan Marsalek, fled and remains a fugitive. In December 2024, Braun was convicted of fraud and sentenced to over eight years in prison.

The German parliamentary inquiry that followed identified what the Bundestag eventually described as a comprehensive regulatory failure. BaFin had repeatedly investigated the wrong party. The German auditing oversight body had failed to identify deficiencies in EY's work. The financial press had been credulous. The political establishment had been protective of a national champion. The short-seller had been right, and had been treated as the problem.

For Perring, Wirecard was vindication. It was also formative. It taught him that the institutional response to credible short reports could be hostile, sustained, and well-resourced — and that the longer the underlying fraud was permitted to grow, the more incentive every defender of it had to attack the messenger. Wirecard's collapse occurred four years after the original Zatarra report. The fraud had grown in those four years, and so had the financial and reputational damage when it eventually unwound.

Perring drew a specific lesson from this. The patterns of fraud are not infinite. They tend to involve the same structural elements: aggressive accounting in areas of executive discretion, regulator defensiveness rather than scrutiny, audit acquiescence, media celebration, and a corporate culture in which dissent is punished and loyalty rewarded. When a short-seller sees these elements together, the underlying business almost always turns out to be other than what it represents itself to be — even if it takes years for the gap to close.

In late 2017, while the Wirecard short was still running and still attracting hostility, Perring was looking at South Africa.

23. Viceroy Research

To the 12 months ended February 2018:

Start Price	Close Price	% Inc.	Market-Cap	Dividends Decl.	NAV / Share
72500c	**83246c**	**14.8%**	**R96,2bn**	**1470c**	**15681c**

By 2017, Perring had begun working with two Australians, Gabriel Bernarde and Aidan Lau, who had been doing their own research on companies they considered overvalued. Bernarde and Lau, based in Melbourne, had come to short-selling through analytical work on TFS Corporation, an Australian sandalwood producer whose accounting they had found questionable. An Australian hedge fund manager[87] who knew both Perring's work and Bernarde and Lau's research made the introduction. The three formed a partnership and incorporated Viceroy Research LLC in the state of Delaware, USA.

Steinhoff International Holdings NV, a South African retail giant, had just announced their intention to purchase Mattress Firm in the United States. Bernarde, Lau, and Perring began to wonder why Steinhoff was making such crazy acquisitions, as Mattress Firm had been on their radar as a potential short. Bernarde, Lau, and Perring began examining Steinhoff in late 2016 and spent most of 2017 working through its financial disclosures across multiple

[87] We haven't been able to confirm who this manager was, but John Hempton is whom we suspect was behind introducing the parties to each other.

jurisdictions. What they found — networks of related-party transactions, off-balance-sheet entities, profit recognition patterns inconsistent with the reported cash generation — was the kind of structural pattern that Wirecard had taught Perring to recognise.[88]

Viceroy had taken a small short position through its prime broker and was several weeks from publishing when, on 5 December 2017, Deloitte refused to sign off on Steinhoff's financial statements. The Steinhoff share price collapsed; CEO Markus Jooste resigned the following day. Viceroy raced to finalise its report and published "Steinhoff's skeletons" — a 37-page report — within hours of Jooste's resignation. It was a bombshell dropped right in the heart of corporate South Africa.

At first, no one knew who Viceroy Research was or who was behind the damning report. Just days after publication, a simple mistake—a photo inserted into the report with metadata that contained Bernarde's name—set the stage for the revealing of their identities.[89] Within days, the short-selling trio was thrust into the public eye, and by Christmas 2017, Viceroy Research was internationally known.

The Steinhoff report had been broadly vindicated by events. Other targets were now being considered. Capitec was among them.

On 19 January 2018, Benguela Global Fund Managers, a Cape Town-based asset manager, sent a letter to Capitec's CFO André du Plessis raising concerns about the bank's treatment of rescheduled

---

[88] Rask Australia (2025), Full Interview with Gabe Bernarde, Australian Investors Podcast, Available at: https://www.youtube.com/ watch?v=TC_PI6W2oas Accessed on: 4 January 2025

[89] Australian journalist, Jonathan Shapiro was the first to pick-up on the metadata and he tracked Bernarde down.

arrear loans. Benguela's analysis suggested that rescheduled arrears were accounting for a significant portion of Capitec's reported loan book growth, that this treatment was distorting the bank's reported performance, and that the practice was potentially indicative of reckless lending. Benguela's letter — measured, professional, technically detailed — was the kind of buy-side concern that, in a healthier disclosure environment, would have prompted clarification from the bank.[90]

Capitec did not significantly change its disclosures in response.

Eleven days later, on the morning of Tuesday, 30 January 2018, at 09h45 South African time, Viceroy Research tweeted a link to its report "Capitec: A Wolf in Sheep's Clothing."[91]

The report ran to thirty-three pages. Its central claims were that Capitec was rolling loans, that rescheduled loans were being reclassified as new loans, that the gross loan book was overstated by between R2.5 billion and R3.1 billion annually across the years 2015 to 2017, and that the bank's reported recoveries were inconsistent with the structure of its lending. The report drew explicit parallels to African Bank, which had collapsed into curatorship in 2014, and called for Capitec to be placed under curatorship to protect depositors and borrowers.

---

[90] Cairns, P (2018), *Benguela Fund Managers: Viceroy is right*. Accessed at: https://www.citizen.co.za/business/benguela-fund-managers-viceroy-is-right/ Accessed on: 30 June 2024

[91] Reports available at https://viceroyresearch.org/capitec-research at the time of writing.

The size of the alleged shortfall — R2.5 to R3.1 billion — is worth dwelling on, because it maps almost exactly onto a figure that Capitec was itself disclosing, if one knew where to look. The footnote treatment described earlier in this book — the recognition of the present value of expected future recoveries within the gross loan book — had been building for years.

By the 2017 financial year, how much did Capitec add to its gross loans and earnings each year by adjusting for the *net present value of expected loan recoveries*? Was it between R2.5 to R3.1 billion? If you searched through the Annual Financial Statements, the only hint that you would get to confirm that Capitec still practised these non-conventional accounting practises was buried in the footnotes.[92]

Viceroy had simply misdiagnosed the source of the discrepancy. Where Viceroy saw loan rolling and rescheduled loans being reclassified as new advances, the actual mechanism was a series of accounting entries that recognised future recoveries on previously written-off loans as present-day assets. The numerical gap that Viceroy identified was real. The technical explanation was different.

The institutional response to the report was rapid and substantially in Capitec's favour. The Reserve Bank issued a statement within hours confirming that Capitec was "solvent and well-capitalised." CEO Gerrie Fourie and CFO André du Plessis appeared on television by midday, describing the Viceroy report as "factually flawed and sensationalist." Intellidex,[93] a research firm commissioned by

---

[92] Capitec's 2013 AFS pg. 117; Capitec's 2014 AFS pg. 123; Capitec's 2015 AFS pg. 132

[93] The research was commissioned by Business Leadership SA, who received a more than ample donation from Capitec Bank prior to commissioning the report.

Capitec, would within days produce a detailed rebuttal arguing that Capitec was operationally distinct from African Bank.

Other evidence of how seriously Capitec was taking the Viceroy report, in the weeks after publicly dismissing it, came from inside the bank. On 8 February 2018, nine days after Viceroy's original report, Capitec issued an internal communication to branch managers under the heading "Change to the Maximum Number of Credit Products per Client." The change was effective the same day. The maximum number of credit products per client was now limited to five — a maximum of four term loans, plus a credit card or credit facility. The communication, leaked to Viceroy and subsequently published in their follow-up, noted that "system changes will be done in future to alert employees granting credit that the maximum number of term loans have been exceeded." Viceroy's reading of the language was that the previous absence of such a system implied that the maximum had not been operationally enforced at branch level before the change. Capitec's reply, when pressed, did not engage the question of what the prior practice had been. What the bank did not do, in either direction, was disclose the policy change publicly. A material adjustment to the bank's credit granting policy, made within ten days of the Viceroy report, was communicated only internally — to the branches, by the bank, by way of internal alert. The market learned of it because the alert was leaked.

Several weeks after the report, on 20 February 2018, Viceroy wrote to Capitec's board of directors with seven specific questions. Capitec's Financial Director, André du Plessis, replied two days later in a letter on the company's letterhead. The reply was made public only because Viceroy subsequently published it. On the credit facility products — the Access Facility, the credit card — Du Plessis wrote: "If the client falls into arrears and then pays up the arrears, where after the client makes a drawdown or a purchase, we legally cannot stop the client doing so. This is a standard feature for credit providers and we estimate the risk of this occurrence when we grant the credit."

The credit ouroboros mechanism described in earlier chapters — the structural feature of the facility product that allows a borrower to repay an arrears balance and immediately redraw the same amount, deferring the default that would otherwise crystallise — was the bank's own description of how its products worked, set out under the signature of the man responsible for the bank's financial reporting. Capitec's rebuttal focused, with considerable force, on the technical explanation Viceroy had offered. It did not address the gap itself, because the gap was already on the balance sheet — disclosed, audited, and accounted for in ways the casual reader of the financial statements would not have detected.

Notwithstanding, the FSCA slapped Viceroy Research and its partners with a R50 million administrative penalty. This was for breaching Section 81 of the Financial Markets Act (FMA) by publishing their infamous 2018 report. The FSCA ruled that the report contained false, misleading, and deceptive statements that caused Capitec's share price to plunge by over 23%, while Viceroy financially benefited via an arrangement with a hedge fund shorting the stock.

It is true that by 11:46 on that Tuesday morning in January 2018, Capitec's share price had fallen from R920 to an intraday low of R705

— a decline of more than 23%. What is not stated, is that by close of business, the share price had recovered to R915, leaving Capitec down less than 3% for the day.

The structural distinctions Intellidex drew in their report were real but partial. African Bank, in its final year, had derived roughly 80% of its revenue from insurance premiums and furniture sales rather than net interest. Capitec, in the period under review, derived its income primarily from net interest, fees, and recoveries. African Bank had no transactional banking; Capitec was the largest retail bank in the country by client numbers. African Bank had no deposit base; Capitec had a significant and growing one. The Intellidex report emphasised these differences and concluded that comparisons between the two banks were misplaced.[94]

What the Intellidex report did not address — and what Viceroy, to its credit, had identified, even if it had not fully understood the mechanism — was the question of how Capitec was treating future recoveries on its written-off loans.

Capitec, at the time of the Viceroy report, had not yet adopted IFRS 9. Under the prior framework, the bank was recognising the present value of expected future recoveries as additions to its gross loan book. This treatment increased reported assets and supported reported earnings without requiring the offsetting recognition of expected future credit losses that IFRS 9 would later require. In 2016, this treatment had added R442 million to gross loans. In 2017, R525 million. In 2018, R906 million — roughly equivalent to the bank's

[94] Theobald, S, Kruger, G, et al., (2018), Investment Research in the Era of Fake News, Intellidex.

annual headline earnings growth for the period. The disclosure was buried in the footnotes: "The estimated recoveries on longer-term loans discounted at the contractual rates are recognised in gross loans and advances."[95] PwC, as auditor, had required the disclosure but not — as far as the public record indicates — a different treatment.

Viceroy had been correct in observing that something in Capitec's gross loan book numbers did not reconcile against new loan sales. They had been wrong about the mechanism. They had thought Capitec was rolling loans; the bank was, in effect, recognising future recoveries in the present.

The Viceroy report's broader institutional point — that Capitec sat within the same Stellenbosch network as Steinhoff, with overlapping figures including Wiese, Mouton, and Jooste — was factually correct and analytically important. But it was the technical accusation about loan rolling that the Capitec response was able to rebut most easily, because the technical accusation was wrong in its specifics even where it was seemingly right in its instinct.

The South African Reserve Bank's intervention — describing Capitec as "solvent and well-capitalised" within hours of the report's release — was the kind of regulator reflex that Perring had seen at BaFin two years earlier. It is the regulator's job to provide reassurance during a market panic; it is not the regulator's job to validate the financial reporting of the institution under question. The two functions are easily conflated, and were conflated here. The Reserve

[95] Capitec's 2015 AFS pg. 141

Bank did not, at any point in the period that followed, conduct or publish a substantive investigation into Viceroy's specific claims about the gross loan book.

Capitec's share price continued to rise. A month after the report, the bank announced headline earnings growth guidance of 16% to 19%, and the share price moved sharply upward. The political backdrop helped: Jacob Zuma resigned the presidency in mid-February 2018, Cyril Ramaphosa was elected in his place, and the rand strengthened on the expectation of reform.

Viceroy published a follow-up report — "A rolling stone gathers no loss"[96] — addressing the responses from SARB, Capitec, and others. The follow-up was less impactful than the original, and by mid-2018 the short trade was running heavily against Viceroy. Fahmi Quadir of Safkhet Capital, who had publicly disclosed a short position in "one of the largest subprime lenders in South Africa," and John Hempton of Bronte Capital, also short, both held their positions but spoke publicly about the cost of being short a stock whose price was rising on the broader market re-rating. Hempton's observation at the time captured the dynamic: "The more persuasively your target lies, the more disconnected from reality the stock price can become."[97]

When IFRS 9 took effect in 2019, the adjustments were material. Capitec's retained earnings were reduced by R950 million on adoption. The capital adequacy ratio fell by 0.5%. Reported profits

---

[96] Reports available at https://viceroyresearch.org/capitec-research at the time of writing.

[97] Poljak, V, Shapiro, J. (2018) 'Behind the rise of activist short sellers', Australian Financial Review. Available at: https://www.afr.com/markets/behind-the-rise-of-activist-short-sellers-20180327-h0xzzi Accessed on: 14 January 2025.

came in lower under the new impairment methodology than they would have under the old. The bank presented the transition as evidence of its conservative approach to risk. The numbers, more accurately, reflected the closure of a treatment that had supported earnings for the better part of a decade.

By the end of February 2019, Capitec had 11.4 million clients and a market capitalisation of R151 billion. The Viceroy report had not stopped the bank's growth. It had not, by any measure available to the public, even slowed it.

For Viceroy, the consequences were more severe. Evidently the Financial Sector Conduct Authority found that Viceroy had a profit-sharing arrangement with Oasis Asset Management — a $10,000 monthly retainer plus 12.5% of net profit on positions taken in response to Viceroy's reports. The FSCA estimated Viceroy's share of Oasis's profits on the Capitec short at approximately $744,482. Viceroy disputed the calculation. The matter remains the subject of ongoing legal challenge.

Viceroy challenged the R50 million fine from the FSCA at the Financial Services Tribunal (FST) and surprisingly enough, in a majority decision in November 2022, the fine was set aside. Refusing to back down, the FSCA launched a review application in the Pretoria High Court to challenge the Tribunal's loophole. On July 9, 2025, the High Court handed down a milestone judgment in favor of the FSCA and effectively remitted the application back to the Financial Services Tribunal (FST) to rule on the fine, knowing that the FSCA does have jurisdiction over Viceroy, and its partners, although they aren't South African domiciled.

The Wirecard collapse came in June 2020, two years and four months after the Capitec report. Perring's central allegations against Wirecard, made in early 2016, were absolutely vindicated. His central allegations against Capitec — that the loan book reporting was unreliable and that the institutional environment around the bank discouraged proper scrutiny — were neither vindicated nor refuted. They were left, by Capitec's settlement of the most serious related challenges and by the FSCA's action against Viceroy, in a state of unresolved disputation. Perring would later describe the FSCA action as confirming, more than rebutting, the institutional thesis of the original report.

24. Close Friends

To the 12 months ended February 2019:

Start Price	Close Price	% Inc.	Market-Cap	Dividends Decl.	NAV / Share
83246c	**130621c**	**57%**	**R151bn**	**1750c**	**18676c**

Jean Pierre Verster had seen this kind of bank before.

In 2012, working as an analyst at 36ONE Asset Management, Verster identified what he believed to be a fundamental disconnect between African Bank's reported performance and the underlying data. "CEO Leon Kirkinis and the board at the time were not in touch with reality," he would later say. "The data was not supporting the narrative."[98]

A 2016 report commissioned by the South African Reserve Bank into African Bank's collapse would attribute the failure to Kirkinis's hubris and the board's loss of grip on credit risk. The Public Investment Corporation, in its own assessment, cited overly aggressive lending and weak risk management. Deloitte, the bank's auditor, would carry some of the regulatory consequences.

[98] Interview conducted by Bruce Whitfield for The Moneymakers on CNBC Africa. Available at: https://www.youtube.com/watch?v=b0XMk6B9Iw4 Accessed on: 23 September 2024.

Verster, then in his early thirties, was already building a reputation as one of the more capable short-sellers or short-sell analysts in South African asset management. A Chartered Accountant with additional CFA and CAIA qualifications,[99] Verster combined statistical analysis with fundamental intuition — a hybrid approach he called "quantamental" modelling. The phrase has since been borrowed widely; in 2012 it was newer. The underlying observation was older: that the financial statements of a deteriorating company often reveal the deterioration before management is willing to acknowledge it, but only to readers who know what they are looking for.

When African Bank collapsed in 2014, the 36ONE funds for which Verster was an analyst recorded more than R100 million in profit on their combined short equity and long debt positions. The position had been built years earlier on a thesis the broader market had ignored. It was vindicated, in the way short positions usually are, only by an event that wiped out the alternative.

In 2014, Verster moved to Fairtree Capital. The move was understood within the industry to be an interim arrangement while he waited for the FSCA[100] to approve his own hedge fund, Protea Capital Management. He would eventually receive that licence and build Protea into one of the more respected smaller managers in the country.

---

[99] CFA - Chartered Financial Analyst; CAIA - Chartered Alternative Investment Analyst
[100] Financial Sector Conduct Authority

Verster had also seen, before most others, the structural problems at Steinhoff. As with African Bank, the market took some time to come around to his view. The pattern, by his own account, recurred in his work: identifying the gap between reported performance and underlying reality early, holding the position through extended periods of disagreement with consensus, and being eventually proven correct by an event the bank, the regulator, the auditor, and the media had collectively failed to anticipate.

It was against this background that, on 23 March 2015, Verster was appointed to the boards of Capitec Bank Holdings and Capitec Bank, and to the chairmanship of the bank's audit committee.

The appointment was unusual. Verster was a short-seller in a culture that did not generally invite short-sellers into the room. He was thirty-four years old and chairing the audit committee of a bank with a market capitalisation already approaching R50 billion. He had no prior banking executive experience. His public profile, to the extent that he had one, was built on calling out the kinds of practices that bank audit committees are supposed to prevent.

The terms of the appointment were modest by listed-company standards. His remuneration was R100,000 a month. He received 5,000 shares with no further option allocation. In November 2019, with Capitec's share price near a record high, he sold his entire allocation for R7.2 million.

The reasons for the appointment, on Capitec's side, have not been publicly explained beyond standard governance language. There are two readings, both of which can be held simultaneously. The charitable reading is that Capitec's board recognised the value of an analyst with Verster's track record of reading financial statements with rigour, and wanted that capability in the room where the bank's own statements were being signed off. The less charitable reading is suggested by the old adage about keeping enemies closer than friends. A man who had been short African Bank and Steinhoff was, on paper, exactly the kind of analyst who might next turn his attention to Capitec. Inviting him onto the audit committee neutralised that possibility, at least for as long as he served. Both readings are consistent with the public record.

I do not know which reading is correct. The most likely answer is that both contain elements of truth — that Capitec's board could see analytical value in Verster's presence and could also see the strategic value of having him bound by the duties of a non-executive director rather than free to publish on the bank from outside it. Boards make this kind of dual-purpose appointment all the time. Verster's tenure on the board did, at minimum, ensure that one of South Africa's most capable corporate sceptics was inside the tent during the years when Capitec's accounting was most aggressive.

When Viceroy Research published its report on Capitec in January 2018, Verster had been chair of the audit committee for nearly three years.

He was, by the public record, the single most qualified individual on the Capitec board to evaluate Viceroy's specific claims. He was a Chartered Accountant. He had personally identified the African Bank and Steinhoff issues. He knew, professionally, what financial statement manipulation looked like. He would have understood, in technical detail, the question of how Capitec was treating estimated future recoveries on written-off loans — the treatment, described elsewhere in this book, that had added approximately R3 billion to the gross loan book by 2017 and was discontinued only when IFRS 9 made continuation impossible.

What Verster said publicly in defence of Capitec during and after the Viceroy episode did not address that treatment. His public statements addressed Viceroy's specific allegations of loan rolling, the comparisons to African Bank, and the institutional credibility of Capitec's governance. These were defensible positions on the specific points Viceroy had raised. They did not engage the broader question of whether Capitec's reported loan book was supported by the underlying economics — a question Verster, of all people, would have been equipped to answer.

This is not an accusation. A non-executive director's duties to the company include the protection of confidential information. Verster could not, while serving on the board, publicly discuss accounting choices he disagreed with internally. If he had disagreed with the recoveries treatment and pressed the audit committee to revise it, he could not have said so publicly. If he had agreed with the treatment as within the standards then applicable, he was under no obligation to volunteer that view either. What the public got was silence on the specific point where his expertise would have mattered most.

A short comparison is instructive. In March 2019, Verster wrote to the board of African Phoenix Investments — the listed successor entity to African Bank Investments Limited — raising concerns about the treatment of dissenting preference shareholders in a proposed scheme of arrangement. The letter was direct. It used the metaphor of a smooth road requiring a "small toll payment" versus a winding, pothole-ridden alternative. It accused African Phoenix's CEO, Gary Shayne, of "extortion" in the structuring of the toll. It warned that failure to resolve the matter would result in protracted conflict.

The letter was the work of a man unafraid to confront a listed company in writing on a matter of principle. Verster was right on the underlying point — the dissenting shareholders' position was eventually vindicated — and the personal cost was significant. In 2023, after years of intervening dispute, Shayne filed a criminal complaint against Verster relating to the language of the 2019 letter. The complaint was the kind of consequence that a director or analyst willing to speak directly to a listed company must, in South Africa, expect to absorb.

The contrast is the chapter's analytical point. Verster, from outside Capitec, would write that kind of letter to African Phoenix's board. From inside Capitec's board, he wrote nothing of the kind — at least not in any form that reached the public record. The recoveries treatment continued. The Viceroy short was attacked. The FSCA fined Viceroy R50 million. The bank's share price continued to rise.

Verster sold his Capitec shares in November 2019 for R7.2 million — a return of approximately fourteen times the original allocation. The sale was not concealed; it appeared on SENS, as required. By any reasonable measure, Capitec's shares were expensive at that level, and the natural reading is that Verster saw better uses for the capital in Protea, which by that point had its FSCA licence and was building its track record. I find nothing peculiar in the timing. A man who has thoroughly absorbed the lessons of African Bank and Steinhoff is, by definition, a man unlikely to hold an over-valued bank share through the eventual mean reversion.

He served on the board for a further four and a half years. He stepped down as a non-executive director in May 2024, observing what he described as a personal cooling-off period and declining to comment publicly on the bank. King IV recommends a maximum of nine years for non-executive independence; Verster had served just over nine. People who have spoken with him privately since report that he continues to regard Capitec as a quality business, even a year after his departure. He is, as ever, entitled to his view.

The question that hovers over the chapter is whether Verster's presence on the Capitec board protected the bank from scrutiny it might otherwise have received. The honest answer is that it probably did, in two ways. First, by reassuring investors that an analyst of his standing was sitting on the audit committee — a signal the market reads as confirmation that the financials are sound. Second, by removing from circulation the one South African analyst most likely, on his prior record, to publish a sceptical thesis on the bank. Neither of these effects requires any impropriety on Verster's part. Both follow naturally from the appointment itself.

There is a version of corporate governance in which this is the system working as intended: bringing capable sceptics inside the room where their scepticism can sharpen the company's decisions. There is another version in which the appointment of a known sceptic to a high-profile board role is the corporate equivalent of buying the journalist. Capitec's board has not explained which version it had in mind, and Verster has not said. The factual content of his public statements during the Viceroy period is consistent with both interpretations.

In finance, history rhymes more than it repeats. Verster has watched Capitec from within for nine years and now watches it from the sidelines. Whether he spotted issues before joining the board, only he knows. Whether his appointment served Capitec's interests or the public's — or, as is most often the case, served both unequally — only those who offered the directorship can really say. The rest of us are left with the public record, which contains everything except the explanation.

25. Alternative Truth

To the 12 months ended February 2020:

Start Price	Close Price	% Inc.	Market-Cap	Dividends Decl.	NAV / Share
130621c	**129999c**	**-0.5%**	**R150.3bn**	**755c**	**22061c**

The pandemic was the first real test of Capitec's loan book. The country went into 'hard lockdown' in late March 2020. Within weeks, large parts of the formal economy stopped paying their staff. Within months, the informal economy had stopped paying anyone. Capitec's customers — millions of them on the lower rungs of the South African labour market — were exactly the cohort whose income disappeared first.

Bad debts rose by 75%, to R7.8 billion. Each percentage point in that figure represents thousands of families choosing between groceries and a loan instalment. Stage 3 loans — the ones the bank itself considers credit-impaired — rose from 11.2% to 13.5% of the book. Headline earnings fell from R6.3 billion to R4.6 billion, a drop of 27%.

Capitec's response was the kind of move that looks either inspired or desperate, depending on what happens next. The bank offered customers who had taken a payment break a refund. Make six consecutive payments after the break and Capitec would refund half the interest charged during it. Make twelve and the bank would refund all of it. The framing was generosity. The reality was risk management. A customer who has accepted a payment break is, statistically, on a path to default. A customer who is making payments — even payments structured around the promise of a future refund — is a customer whose loan is not being written off. The refund offer was the cheaper outcome for the bank.

The same logic, on a larger scale, drove what Capitec did with its product mix. Term loans had been the bread and butter of Capitec's credit business. In 2021 the bank cut its term loan book roughly in half, from R28.8 billion to R14.3 billion. In May 2020 it had launched the Access Facility, a revolving credit product that disbursed R6.4 billion in its first ten months.

The Access Facility is, in form, a credit facility of up to R500,000 against which a customer can draw and repay as needed. In practice it is a treadmill. There is nothing to prevent a customer from depositing a repayment into the Access Facility and immediately drawing the same amount back out. The loan is technically being serviced. The default that would otherwise have been crystallised is technically not happening. As long as the customer has any cash flow at all — a remittance, a piece of informal work, a pension grant — the loan does not need to fall into arrears. It does not need to be written off. It does not need to appear in the provisioning.

This is the genius of the product, if you are running the bank. It defers the moment of recognition almost indefinitely. The customer is, by every accounting measure, in good standing. The bank is, by every accounting measure, well-provisioned. The only thing that has actually happened is that the loan has been moved from a category in which it would have been written off into a category in which it will not be.

By the year to February 2022, recoveries had fallen by 26%, from R1.26 billion to R932 million, and then to R815 million the following year. 2022.[101] The total value of loans disbursed fell by 25% over the same period. The pandemic was constricting Capitec's ordinary business at the same time as the Access Facility was offering an alternative. The bank had room to manoeuvre, and it manoeuvred.

It was in this context, in September 2021, that the Financial Sector Conduct Authority chose to make a point.

Commissioner Unathi Kamlana stood in front of the press in Pretoria and announced that the FSCA was imposing administrative penalties totalling R50 million on Viceroy Research, the small overseas research firm whose January 2018 report had briefly knocked 23% off Capitec's share price before the share recovered. "In January 2018, Viceroy Research published a report," Kamlana said. He paused. "A report that caused the share price to plummet 27% in a single day." The facts were that it dropped 23%, and then recovered on the day, still he continued. "While this happened, Viceroy Research were profiting from their misinformation. The founders of Viceroy, Messrs. Lau, Perring, and Bernarde, knew — or ought to have reasonably known — that the information was false. Further, notwithstanding being made aware that their publication was untrue, they failed to publish complete and frank corrections, as required."

Kamlana went on to refer to Viceroy's findings as the "alternative truth" a term that Perring finds amusing to this day and a term that

---

[101] Recoveries continued to drop to R642 million in 2023 and to R498 million in 2024.

reinforces the notion that "truth" is relative and often a matter of perspective.

The action was unprecedented. A South African regulator was, more than three and a half years after the fact, fining a foreign research firm for the contents of a published report on a JSE-listed bank. The size of the penalty — R50 million — had no obvious comparator in the FSCA's prior practice. The timing, in the middle of a pandemic during which Capitec's reported numbers were being held up by a product whose function was to defer defaults, was either coincidence or it was not.

Kamlana said that he had "tested all allegations the short-seller made by referring back to the 2018 financial statements," and that he hoped the decision would "be a deterrent to those hoping to make a quick buck by peddling false information." Anyone with any savvy would have known that the 2018 financial statements came out approximately two months after the Viceroy Research report and if Kamlana was really interested in the truth, then he would have been looking into earlier financial statements.

Nothing in the Viceroy report on Capitec was false. The report drew conclusions from publicly disclosed information; some of those conclusions, as discussed in the previous chapter, identified the right gap in the loan book but offered the wrong mechanism to explain it. Drawing the wrong conclusion from accurate information is not the same as peddling false information. Kamlana, in his own statement, described the standard as what Viceroy "knew or ought to have reasonably known" — a formulation that does the analytical work of converting an interpretive disagreement into a regulatory offence.

If Kamlana had been reviewing Capitec's 2018 financial statements and the prior statements with the rigour he claimed, he might have noticed something else. In the year to February 2018, Capitec's provision for bad debts had fallen by 37%. In the same year, write-offs had risen by 37%. Provisions and write-offs do not normally move in opposite directions of the same magnitude. When they do, there is usually a story underneath the numbers. The story, in Capitec's case, was the one the previous chapter described: the recognition of estimated future recoveries within the gross loan book, building toward what would become the R950 million reduction in retained earnings on the adoption of IFRS 9 a year later. The treatment was within the standards then applicable. It was not within the spirit of conservative banking provisioning. Viceroy had been wrong about the mechanism but right about the gap.

Kamlana's certainty about Capitec's 2018 financial statements becomes more interesting when one notices where Kamlana had been working when those statements were published.

In July 2015, Nkosana Mashiya, then the Deputy Registrar of Banks at the South African Reserve Bank, resigned. Kamlana stepped into the role and was eventually formally appointed as his successor. He served as Deputy Registrar of Banks from 2016 to 2018. Mashiya, having left the SARB, was at the time of the Viceroy report a non-executive director of Capitec Bank. When Viceroy published in January 2018, Kamlana was the Deputy Registrar of Banks at the central bank that, within hours, issued the public statement describing Capitec as "solvent and well-capitalised." Kamlana — by then Commissioner of the FSCA — fined Viceroy for having questioned the financial statements of a bank on whose board his former boss sat, and which his other former boss, the Regulator of Banks, had moved quickly to defend.

There is no suggestion of impropriety here. South African banking regulation is conducted by a small number of people who have known each other for a long time. Movement between the SARB, the FSCA, the National Treasury, and the boards of regulated banks is common and unremarkable. The University of Stellenbosch confers honorary doctorates on regulators with some regularity. The same names recur. The same relationships persist. None of this is, in itself, evidence of anything other than the smallness of South Africa's financial regulatory community.

It is, however, the context in which the Viceroy fine was levied. A foreign research firm published a critical report on a JSE-listed bank in January 2018. The Reserve Bank publicly defended the bank within hours. Local research firms produced commissioned rebuttals within days. The bank's share price recovered within hours and continued to rise. Three and a half years later, at the tail end of a pandemic during which the bank's reported performance was being supported by a product whose function was to defer the recognition of defaults, the FSCA fined the foreign research firm R50 million.[102]

The formal rule says that regulators protect depositors, ensure systemic stability, and act without fear or favour. The informal rule says that the regulators are members of the same small professional community as the regulated, that they move between roles within that community over the course of their careers, and that the institutions they regulate today are the institutions they may sit on the boards of tomorrow. Both rules operate simultaneously.

Bank failures are caused, almost without exception, by the people who are supposed to prevent them. Executives mistake risk for opportunity. Risk officers mistake market expansion for innovation. Regulators mistake reassurance for oversight. When the cycle is favourable, the executives extract their bonuses. When the cycle turns, the executives have already converted their equity to cash and exited the building. The customers, the depositors, the minority shareholders, and the public are left holding the loan book.

The regulators, generally, are not blamed for this. They were doing their job, which they understand as preventing panic, maintaining confidence, and ensuring orderly markets. The job they did not do, in this telling, was the one that would have required them to question the financial reporting of a major institution at the moment when questioning it was unwelcome.

---

[102] Apparently they contravended Section 81(1), (2) of the Financial Markets Act 19 of 2012.

To the 12 months ended February 2021:

Start Price	Close Price	% Inc.	Market-Cap	Dividends Decl.	NAV / Share
129999c	**133875c**	**3%**	**R154.8bn**	**1600c**	**25824c**

Capitec claims more than 25 million clients[103] in a country of 63 million people[104], of which only 7.4 million are taxpayers and 29 million are social grant recipients—four for every taxpayer.[105] The unemployment rate, on the official measure, is 32.9%. Most holders of a Capitec bank card are therefore either a grant recipient or someone the state classifies as unemployed. This is not an accusation. It is the demographic reality of a country in which the formal economy is small and the bank that serves the rest of the population is, by definition, the bank that serves the people the formal economy has not absorbed.

---

[103] As at end of February 2026.

[104] Statistics South Africa Accessed at: https://www.statssa.gov.za/?p=17430 Accessed on: 20 October 2024

[105] BusinessTech, *29 million people on grants in South Africa – but only 7.4 million taxpayers,* Accesssed at: https://businesstech.co.za/news/finance/798152/29-million-people-on-grants-in-south-africa- but-only-7-4-million-taxpayers/ Accessed on: 20 November 2024

In June 2025, Capitec's CEO Gerrie Fourie was asked about the unemployment rate. "Stats SA doesn't count self-employed people," he said. "I think that's an area we need to correct. The unemployment rate is probably actually 10%. Just go look at the number of people in the township informal market, who are selling all sorts of stuff, who have a turnover of R1,000 a day."[106]

The quote is worth pausing on. The official unemployment rate is one of the most contested statistics in South African public life, and Fourie is offering an estimate that is roughly a third of the official number. He is, in effect, arguing that Capitec's market is much larger and much more economically active than the conventional read of the country's economy suggests. Whether he is right is a separate question. What matters here is that Capitec's strategy reflects this view. The bank is built for the South Africa Fourie describes: a population in which informal income is widespread, cash is still central, and physical presence is what makes a bank usable. Whether that South Africa survives the next decade is the question on which the bank's future depends.

The pricing tells the same story. The average Capitec customer pays R48 a month in fees. The average customer at one of the Big Four pays R247. The product range is

---

[106] Kumalo, K(2025), Capitec CEO argues SA's jobless rate as low as 10%, Business Day, Available at: https://www.businesslive.co.za/bd/economy/2025-06-10-capitec-ceo-argues-sas-jobless-rate-as-low-as-10/ Accessed on: 10 June 2025

deliberately limited. The branches are designed to be cheap to operate. Lines outside Capitec branches in major centres are routine, and the customers in those lines have, broadly, decided that the trade-off is worth it: longer waits in exchange for fees that are roughly one-fifth of what the alternatives charge.

On every measure that mattered to Capitec's growth through the 2010s, the strategy worked. The bank moved from a microlender at the periphery of the system to the largest retail bank in the country by client numbers. The brand became, for millions of South Africans, the first bank account they had ever held. The customer loyalty is real and well-earned.

It is also, possibly, the wrong loyalty for the next decade.

Capitec's competitors have spent the past five years closing branches and removing ATMs. Between 2019 and 2024, the total number of ATMs operated by South African banks fell by 13%. Over the same period, Capitec's ATM count rose by 67%. By 2024, Capitec was running 75% more ATMs than FirstRand — the country's largest bank by assets — and operating 42% more branches than any of the Big Four. The industry was contracting physical infrastructure. Capitec was expanding it.

Fourie defends the strategy in terms that are coherent on their own. Branches build trust. Cash remains essential in the informal economy. The customer Capitec serves is not the customer who will adopt a fully digital bank tomorrow. None of this is wrong. The question is whether it stays right.

TymeBank, founded in 2019 as a fully digital bank, had reached 10 million customers by 2024. Discovery Bank, also digital-first, has built a smaller but higher-income base. The combined client numbers of the two are still less than half of Capitec's. Neither is, in any conventional sense, threatening Capitec's core market. What they are doing is establishing that a South African retail bank can be operated without physical infrastructure at a meaningful scale — something the Big Four's legacy cost structures could not previously demonstrate.

To the 12 months ended February 2022:

Start Price	Close Price	% Inc.	Market-Cap	Dividends Decl.	NAV / Share
133875c	**207435c**	**55%**	**R240.8bn**	**3640c**	**30888c**

In the summer of 2004, executives of a fledgling DVD-by-mail company called Netflix walked into the gleaming headquarters of Blockbuster Entertainment. They proposed that Blockbuster purchase Netflix for $50 million.[107] The Blockbuster executives—titans of an empire spanning 9,000 stores across the globe—barely suppressed their laughter. Here was this upstart with his ridiculous red envelopes, suggesting he could replace the Friday night ritual of wandering the aisles of America's favourite video store. They showed the Netflix execs the door. Today, Netflix is

[107] Marc Randolph and Reed Hastingsflew to Dallas, Texas, only to be dismissed.

worth $386 billion. Some might argue that Capitec is analogous with Netflix, others might argue that they are a Blockbuster, expanding their empire.

The retail banking analogy to Blockbuster,[108] much used in commentary, is imperfect. Banking is not video rental. The product is bundled, regulated, sticky, and protected by switching frictions that Blockbuster never had. The displacement of physical-network banking by digital banking, if it happens, will take decades rather than years. Banks tend to acquire their disrupters rather than be killed by them. None of this means the displacement does not happen. It means the displacement happens slowly enough that the displaced institution can convince itself, for a long time, that it is winning. Still, I do see problems with building branch infrastructure of bricks-and-mortar when the landscape is changing to digital, away from physical stores.

The more useful framework is Clayton Christensen's innovator's dilemma. A successful incumbent, having built a business that serves its existing customers well, faces a structural problem when a lower-margin alternative emerges. The incumbent's existing customers do not initially want the alternative. The incumbent's existing cost structure makes competing with the alternative unprofitable. By the time the alternative has

[108] Naysmith, C (2023), *Blockbuster Had The Opportunity To Buy Netflix For $50 Million But 'Laughed Them Out Of The Room' — A $150 Billion Mistake* Accessed at: https://finance.yahoo.com/news/blockbuster-had-opportunity-buy-netflix-185915158.html Accessed on: 19 November 2024

improved enough to be attractive to the incumbent's customers, the incumbent has lost the cost discipline required to match it. The incumbent does not fail because it is poorly managed. It fails because it is well-managed for the wrong question.

Capitec's cost trajectory is the data point that matters most. In 2024, operating expenses rose 14%. In the first half of 2025, they rose 30%. FirstRand, over the same period, contained its cost growth to 5%. The bank that built its reputation on cost discipline is now growing costs faster than its larger competitors — at a moment when the smaller, fully-digital entrants are growing without the cost base at all.

There are two readings of this. The first is that Capitec is investing ahead of the curve — building the infrastructure, the staff capability, and the product range required to capture business banking, insurance, and the higher-margin segments the bank has historically not served. The second is that Capitec is doubling down on a strategy whose marginal returns are already falling. Both readings can be true simultaneously. The question is which dominates.

The customers who stood loyally in those long branch lines, proud of their Capitec cards and the fees they saved against the Big Four, may discover over the next decade that the bank they trusted has, in pursuing growth, become more expensive to run and more similar to the institutions it disrupted. The same customers may also discover that they do not need to stand in branch lines at all — that a phone, a national ID number, and a

TymeBank account (now called GoTyme) does the job at one-tenth of the operational cost to the bank.

This is the central paradox of Capitec's current position. The bank that built itself on radical simplicity is adding complexity. The populist movement that took clients from the incumbents is now pursuing upmarket profits. The cost discipline that defined the early years is loosening at exactly the moment when the digital entrants are establishing what the new cost benchmark looks like. GoTyme's customer acquisition cost is under $5 per new client, reportedly the lowest in the industry.[109]

None of this is a prediction. Capitec may navigate the transition successfully. Its scale, its brand, and its data on 24.1 million customers are real advantages that no fully-digital entrant can match in the short term. The bank's leadership is not unaware of the question. Fourie has been explicit about business banking as the next growth engine, and the IT investment line in recent results suggests that the digital build is being taken seriously.

What is also true is that the most dangerous moment in a successful business is the one in which success makes change feel optional. The incumbents Capitec disrupted in the 2000s had every reason, on the metrics they were watching, to believe their position was secure. The metrics Capitec is now watching are, in

[109] Saville, A, Whitfield, B (2025), It's About Tyme Banking Beyond Borders, MacMillan, pg. 27

their own way, equally encouraging. The question is whether the metrics being watched are the metrics that matter.[110] [111] [112] [113] [114]

To the 12 months ended February 2023:

Start Price	Close Price	% Inc.	Market-Cap	Dividends Decl.	NAV / Share
207435c	**175451c**	**-15.4%**	**R203.7bn**	**4200c**	**33760c**

[110] Accessed at: https://bankingtransformationafrica.com/south-african-banks-atm-strategies-closures-and-innovations-amid-digital-banking-surge/ Accessed on: 20 November 2024

[111] My apologies to Otto von Bismarck

[112] Labuschagne, H (2024) MyBroadband. *South African banks closing ATMs and shrinking branches*. Available at: https://mybroadband.co.za/news/banking/570931-south-african -banks -closing-atms-and-shrinking-branches.html Accessed on: 22 Nov. 2024

[113] Capitec Bank numbers are as at 31 August 2024. Numbers for ABSA, FNB, Standard Bank and Nedbank are as at 30 June 2024 according to financial statements. TymeBank is per commentary in October 2024, 30 June numbers were at 9.75 million. Discovery Bank numbers are from BusinessTech, *Discovery Bank hits 1 million customers in South Africa* Accessed at: https://businesstech.co.za/news/ banking/788226/discovery- bank-hits-1-million -customers-in-south-africa/ Accessed on: 20 November 2024.

[114] Blockbuster's 2004-2007 10-K reports

27. Late Arrival

To the 12 months ended February 2024:

Start Price	Close Price	% Inc.	Market-Cap	Dividends Decl.	NAV / Share
175451c	**201777c**	**15%**	**R234.3bn**	**4875c**	**37611c**

The South African experiment with bancassurance — the cross-selling of insurance products through banking channels — was the defining financial services story of the 1990s and 2000s. Standard Bank acquired Liberty. Absa partnered with Sanlam. Nedbank engaged with Old Mutual. The logic was straightforward. Banks had captive customer bases, transaction data, and distribution networks. Insurers had products, actuarial expertise, and high-margin annuity income. Combining the two, in theory, produced a financial supermarket that captured more of each customer's wallet than either party could on its own.

In practice, the experiment ran into two problems. The first was that the regulated insurance products and the regulated banking products were governed by different supervisory regimes, with different capital treatments, different conduct requirements, and different risk dynamics. The second was that the aggressive cross-selling that made bancassurance profitable also produced exactly the kind of customer outcomes that the post-2008 wave of conduct regulation was designed to prevent. The Financial Advisory and Intermediary Services Act, the Treating Customers Fairly framework, and the requirement for a documented financial needs analysis before product sale together made it significantly harder to sell a financial product to a customer who had walked into a branch for something else.

By the mid-2010s, the bancassurance party was effectively over. The major banks had quietly reduced their cross-selling ambitions. The integration with their insurance partners had not produced the synergies originally projected. The model had not failed, exactly, but it had not delivered what its promoters had promised.

Capitec's entry into insurance dates from this moment. In 2017 the bank began offering credit life cover — the insurance attached to its lending products — through a cell captive structure, a vehicle that allowed it to participate in the underwriting economics of insurance without holding its own insurance licence. The cell captive was, in retrospect, an unusually well-judged structural choice. It gave Capitec the upside of insurance underwriting while keeping the regulatory perimeter narrow and the capital requirements modest. It also, less visibly, gave the bank a way to participate in insurance earnings whose disclosure was less transparent than full-licensed underwriting would have required.

In 2023, Capitec acquired a life insurance licence and established Capitec Life. The cell captive had served its purpose: the bank had built the customer relationships, the data, and the underwriting confidence to operate insurance directly. By the year to February 2025, insurance accounted for 25% of Capitec's total earnings. The bank had, in less than a decade, built an insurance business of material weight to the group.

It had done so by deploying a sales model that the established banks could no longer use. "Assurance is sold and not bought," Fourie tells his recruits, and the phrase carries the entire philosophy. Insurance products do not market themselves. The customer who needs them most is the customer least likely to seek them out. The way to grow an insurance book is to put trained salespeople in front of customers who have come into the branch for something else.

This is the practice that bancassurance regulation in the 2010s was designed to constrain. Capitec's training emphasises the financial needs analysis, the compliance requirements, and the documentation. It also emphasises sales. The training itself has an interesting origin: in Capitec's early days, when branches handled significant volumes of physical cash, somewhere between fifty and a hundred employees were dismissed each year for theft. The original purpose of head office training was to instil the consequences of misappropriation. The skills developed in that context — close supervision of branch staff, structured incentive systems, monitored conversion rates — transferred well to the work of selling insurance products to customers who had come in to deposit a salary.

By 2025, Capitec was carrying 3.3 million insurance policies covering 15 million lives. A quarter of the bank's total revenue was flowing from a product line that, a decade earlier, did not exist on the income statement.

The concentration of this insurance book is worth understanding. The majority of it is credit life cover — the insurance attached to Capitec's lending products, sold at the point of loan origination, paying out if the borrower dies, becomes disabled, or loses their income. Credit life is a regulated product with capped premiums and prescribed payout terms. It is also, by its structure, perfectly correlated with the underlying loan book. A borrower who cannot service a loan is also a borrower who may trigger a credit life claim. The same economic conditions that produce loan defaults produce insurance claims.

This is the structural risk Capitec's insurance growth has built into the business. The diversification away from banking, in earnings terms, is not in fact a diversification of risk. A South African recession that drives up unemployment will simultaneously increase credit impairments in the banking book and increase claims in the insurance book. The two lines that, on the income statement, look like independent earnings streams are, on the underwriting reality, the same earnings stream measured twice.

Capitec's leadership is not unaware of this. The bank's disclosures address credit life concentration. The reinsurance arrangements are presumably structured against extreme tail outcomes. The concern is not that Capitec has overlooked the correlation. The concern is that the reported earnings growth is, in part, a function of writing the same risk twice and counting it in two different places.

The other notable feature of Capitec's insurance growth is its timing. The bancassurance era has ended for almost everyone else. The conduct rules, the FNA requirements, the supervisory expectations — all of these have made it materially harder for the established banks to sell insurance through their branch networks at the volumes they once did. Capitec has built a sales-led insurance business in the regulatory environment that was meant to make sales-led insurance businesses impossible. The bank has done this within the rules. It has also done it by virtue of operating in market segments — lower-income, more cash-dependent, less digitally engaged — where the conduct risks the regulators were most concerned about are still present, just less visible.

The most telling validation of Capitec's model is that Old Mutual, one of the country's largest insurers, is now trying to enter banking. The strategy is essentially the inverse of Capitec's: cross-sell banking services to an existing insurance customer base. Old Mutual tried this before, with Nedbank, and the integration disappointed. The fact that the group is trying again is the clearest possible signal that Capitec's success has reset the strategic question. If a bank can build a 25%-of-earnings insurance business from a starting point of no insurance licence, then perhaps an insurer can build a comparable banking business in reverse. The history of the previous attempt suggests this is harder than it looks. The willingness to try anyway suggests the prize is now considered large enough to justify the cost.

What Capitec's insurance growth represents is not, in the end, the diversification that the headline numbers suggest. It is a doubling-down on the same customer base, sold a second product alongside the first, with the second product's risk correlated to the first. The earnings are real. The growth is real. The 25% contribution to total earnings is real. The structural exposure is also real — and is more concentrated than the line-item disclosure makes it appear.

The bank's future depends, in the end, on the same thing it has always depended on: the health of its loan book. The insurance business, far from offering protection against deterioration in the loan book, is correlated with it. If unemployment rises, if real incomes fall, if the South African consumer cycle turns, both lines respond together. The diversification is on the income statement. It is not in the underlying risk.

28. Getting Business

To the 12 months ended February 2025:

Start Price	Close Price	% Inc.	Market-Cap	Dividends Decl.	NAV / Share
307437c	**201777c**	**52%**	**R357bn**	**6510c**	**43970c**

Capitec's growth in personal credit has decelerated. The Access Facility has stabilised the back book. Insurance has provided new earnings, structurally correlated with the loan book but reported as a separate line. The question for the bank's next decade is where the next leg of growth comes from. The answer Capitec has settled on is business banking.

Business banking currently accounts for 5% of Capitec's total earnings. The segment is growing fast. Active business clients rose 15% in the year to February 2025, to 218,207. Scored loan balances more than doubled, to R1.3 billion. The merchant commerce strategy — selling card machines outright rather than renting them, and offering lower commission rates than the established acquirers — added 124% to the active trading merchant base, which now stands at 63,000 with annual turnover of R64 billion. The Capitec card-swipe sound has become one of the more ubiquitous audio cues in South African retail.

Capitec is doing in business banking what it did in retail: targeting an underserved segment at a lower price point than the established players will match. The minimum monthly fee for a Capitec business account is R50. Bank Zero, the smaller fully-digital competitor, charges nothing. The same dynamic that Capitec used against the Big Four in retail is now being run against Capitec by the next generation of entrants.

The underlying purpose of the business account is the data. Capitec's existing retail data has supported a decade of credit decision-making. The transactional data from 218,207 business accounts is the next layer — the input that allows the bank to offer instant overdrafts, working capital lines, and the longer-duration credit products that small-business lending in South Africa has historically lacked. This is, in principle, a legitimate and useful direction. South African small businesses are under-served by formal credit, and a bank that can underwrite them using transactional data rather than collateral fills a real gap. The difficulty is that the credit-granting practices Capitec has carried into business banking are recognisable from earlier chapters. The same lineage of bankers that built the personal credit book is now extending its approach to the corporate one.

The National Credit Act applies, by default, to every credit agreement in South Africa. Where the lender wants to argue the Act does not apply, the burden is on the lender to establish that the borrower falls within one of the Act's exceptions. The most relevant exception for business banking is the one that excludes companies whose annual turnover exceeds R1 million. The exception is reasonable in principle. Larger businesses, the legislature concluded, do not need the same consumer-style protections as individuals. The question Capitec's business lending raises is what work the lender does, at the moment of granting credit, to satisfy itself that the threshold has actually been met.

At Capitec's 2022 annual results presentation, Gerrie Fourie described the bank's business credit approach plainly: "Business banking was providing credit to people where we just look at their turnover"[115] This is what the bank was doing then, and what it has continued to do. The practical implementation works as follows. Where the credits to a business bank account over a twelve-month period exceed R1 million, Capitec treats the business as falling outside the NCA. The bank then offers the company credit and requires the directors to sign personal suretyships or guarantees, without a full credit application, without independently verified financial statements, and without an underwriting process that would withstand scrutiny in a non-NCA jurisdiction.

South Africa does need banks lending to small businesses. What it does not need is banks that conflate the appearance of turnover with the substance of it, and that use the absence of NCA jurisdiction as an excuse to underwrite less rigorously than is otherwise required. The health of Capitec's business bank loan book depends on the answer to a question the bank has chosen not to ask at origination.

---

[115] The 2022 Results Presentation took place on 12 April 2022, the quote can be heard at approximately 53 mins. Available at: *https://www.youtube.com/watch?v=mFyeww_1N6Y*

A recent matter in the Magistrates' Court of Cape Town illustrates the point. [2154/2022] The defendant, a small business owner who had signed a personal suretyship for his company's Capitec credit facility, cross-examined the bank's relationship manager from the witness box.

The defendant put it to the witness that Capitec had calculated the company's "turnover" simply by adding up the credits to the bank account over twelve months — a figure that, on the bank's totting, exceeded R2 million.

"Are you familiar with the term 'kiting'?" the self-represented defendant asked.

The witness hesitated. The defendant explained: kiting is the practice of moving funds between accounts to inflate the appearance of activity. A credit to a bank account is not necessarily turnover. It may be a capital injection, a loan drawdown, a refund, a transfer from another account held by the same business, or a deliberate inflation of apparent activity. The National Credit Act, at Section 82, requires a credit provider to have appropriate assessment mechanisms in place, including the verification of financial information. Section 4(2)(1) places a positive duty on the credit provider to ask the borrower about stated turnover at the time of granting credit, not before and not after.

The defendant asked the witness to confirm that Capitec had not requested the company's turnover figure, had not asked for financial statements, and had not required a credit application form. The witness confirmed that this was correct.

"How, then, could the bank be certain that the company's actual turnover exceeded R1 million?" the defendant asked.

The witness's answer was that the credits to the account were visible to the bank, and that the credits exceeded the threshold.

The judge ruled for Capitec. The court's reasoning was that, on the facts before it, a reasonable person would have concluded that the company's actual turnover exceeded R1 million. The defendant's substantive point — that Capitec had not done the work at origination that the Act requires — was not the question the court took itself to be answering.

Capitec won the case. The bank did not need to win it on the standard the Act actually sets. It won it on a lower standard — whether, in retrospect and on the documentation available to the court, the threshold had probably been met. That lower standard is the standard the bank's business lending has been operating under all along. The bank does not verify turnover at origination because, in court, it does not need to. The R1 million threshold becomes whatever the credits to the account look like at the moment of dispute, rather than what the directors would have told a credit officer if a credit officer had asked.

The case also illustrates the structural problem with the legal system in South Africa. Most defendants in matters of this kind do not have the resources to cross-examine a bank's loan exposure on the basis of credits to a bank account. Notwithstanding that section 4(2)(a) provides the mechanism for establishing turnover — and its express purpose is to eliminate ambiguity. The legislature used the phrase 'for greater certainty' to introduce the provision:

> *"[F]or greater certainty, the asset value or annual turnover of a juristic person at the time a credit agreement is made, is the value stated as such by that juristic person at the time it applies for or enters into that agreement."*

This provision is unambiguous. The turnover for threshold purposes is not what a bank infers from deposit data. Turnover and deposit data are not the same thing. They have not been since the introduction of double-entry bookkeeping. The fact that they are being treated as the same thing, in a R1.3 billion and rapidly growing business loan book, is the question that hovers over Capitec's next leg of growth. Turnover is also not what a reasonable person might conclude from deposit data. The magistrate was wrong in this ruling. It is the value stated as such by the juristic person at the time it applied for or entered into the specific credit agreement.

In the originary course of events, a debtor who would lose such a case would have the right to appeal the matter in the High Court. If they wanted to defend the matter themselves, Capitec would ask for security, and ordinarily the Court would ask for a deposit of at least R50,000 in the event that the debtor lost the appeal motion. For this reason, many judgments go uncontested and the banks go on to recover those debts by attaching assets or selling the debt to a third party.

29. Value-Added Services

TJ Strydom opens a chapter of his book *Capitec: Stalking Giants* with the line: "Capitec wanted to be a bank, nothing else — and initially, nowhere else other than in South Africa. And it wanted to grant loans and open savings accounts. That was all." Focus, Strydom records, was one of the lessons Jannie Mouton claimed to have learned from the Capitec executives. Mouton has said publicly that in the bank's early years he approached them with suggestions to sell prepaid airtime and funeral policies, and they declined.[116]

The reader of an earlier chapter will recall Key Distributors — the small, largely dormant Capitec subsidiary used in 2002 to manufacture R3.5 million of headline earnings on the eve of the bank's first financial year-end as a listed entity. Key Distributors was incorporated as a fast-moving consumer goods business, intended to distribute essential products to the bank's customers. The FMCG ambition never materialised in physical form. The underlying instinct — to sell non-banking products to a captive banking customer base — did not go away.

The model African Bank pursued in furniture — selling a physical product and financing its purchase, capturing margin on both legs — was the template Capitec briefly considered and then abandoned. What Capitec built instead is a financial supermarket of intangibles: electricity, airtime, data, and insurance. The customer is the same. The captive is the same. The margin is collected without inventory.

[116] Gordan Institute Business School (2014), Jannie Mouton Part 2, Available at: https://www.youtube.com/watch?v=NiClyov_2cc Accessed on: 6 January 2025.

Value Added Services and Capitec Connect, the bank's mobile-virtual-network operation, together generated R4.4 billion in net income in the year to February 2025, up 61% year-on-year and contributing 23% of group earnings. The growth raises an analytical question. The same airtime, data, and electricity sales that Capitec books as high-margin revenue pass through wholesale arrangements with the underlying providers — Blue Label Telecoms, the holding company of Cell C, among them. Blue Label's reported earnings from the same flow of transactions have not grown at anything close to the Capitec rate. Either the margin economics of intermediating these transactions are very different from the underlying provider economics, or the way the two parties book the same flow of revenue is different, or both.

The Capitec app is the channel through which most of this revenue flows. Over 11 million customers use the app for digital purchases — airtime, data, electricity. Capitec claims a market share of more than 40% of South African airtime and data transactions. Capitec Connect, the bank's mobile-virtual-network arm, grew its active SIM base by 74% to 1.6 million subscribers in the year to February 2025, contributing R193 million in net income.

The bank's loan book is almost entirely unsecured. For most of its history, Capitec used third-party providers for credit life cover — the insurance attached to lending that pays out if the borrower dies, becomes disabled, or loses their income. Since acquiring its own assurance licence in 2023, Capitec has progressively brought this underwriting in-house, a structural choice that resembles the integration African Bank pursued before its collapse. A meaningful share of the bank's earnings growth in the last three years has come from selling funeral and credit life policies to its existing customer base. This is, on its own, a defensible commercial strategy. It does, however, concentrate the bank's risk exposure to the South African unsecured consumer in ways the line-item disclosure does not always make obvious.

For several years before the acquisition, Capitec held a 40% stake in a European online lender called Creamfinance, which rebranded as AvaFin shortly before Capitec acquired the remaining 57% in March 2024 for R535 million. The cash went not to AvaFin's balance sheet but to its co-founders, Matīss Ansviesulis and Dāvis Bārons. The terms of the exit, as disclosed, did not preclude the founders from setting up similar online lending operations in other jurisdictions. Capitec acquired the operating business; the founders kept their expertise, their networks, and their proceeds. AvaFin contributed approximately 2% of Capitec's total earnings in the year to February 2025.[117]

Let's step back to discuss the controversy surrounding Creamfinance Poland, which stemmed from a major regulatory crackdown on the company's methods for handling defaults and loan extensions. Instead of litigating directly through standard collection lines, the group utilised a network of interconnected subsidiary entities—such as MDP Finance, KIM Finance, and JJK Credit—to systematically "roll over" consumer debts. When a borrower struggled to repay a

[117]All of these businesses were owned by Ansiesulis and Baron: **money.jo** which provides unsecured and secured consumer loans to citizens of Jordan, **loan.me** provides unsecured consumer loans to Sri Lanka, **Esketit** is a loan crowdfunding platform, **f-u capital** is owners of crypto assets can obtain loans or real-world assets from different companies, **spandu capital** purchases non-performing loans from different institutions, hands it to debt collectors and then makes a margin in-between, inter alia.

short-term loan, they were immediately pushed into successive refinancing loans with a sister company to cover the previous balance, accumulating massive, compounding commission fees each time.[118]

This structural workaround caught the attention of Poland's Office of Competition and Consumer Protection (UOKiK). Following a wave of consumer complaints, UOKiK ruled that this cyclical refinancing structure was an illegal evasion of Poland's statutory caps on non-interest loan costs. The watchdog revealed that borrowers frequently found themselves drowning in several layers of refinancing agreements where the actual cash never changed hands, but the cumulative fees quickly exceeded the original principal amount. Consequently, the regulator handed down severe financial penalties against the group to penalise the practice and enforce strict compliance with Poland's evolving "anti-usury" frameworks.[119]

In Poland, UOKiK's investigation proved that Creamfinance used internal subsidiary entities specifically as a structural workaround to deliberately bypass statutory interest and fee caps.

In South Africa, both Capitec and the South African Reserve Bank (SARB) fiercely rejected Viceroy's accusations which were essentially that Capitec were also refinancing loans. Capitec clarified that they

---

118 Urząd Ochrony Konkurencji i Konsumentów (UOKiK), 2024. Decyzja Prezesa Urzędu Ochrony Konkurencji i Konsumentów nr DOZIK.610.2.2021. Warszawa: UOKiK.

119 Wojewódzki Inspektorat Inspekcji Handlowej w Kielcach (WIIH Kielce), 2024. Pożyczanie pieniędzy – Decyzje Prezesa UOKiK [online]. Available at: https://www.wiihkielce.pl/komunikaty-uokik/ 640-pozyczanie-pieniedzy-decyzje-prezesa-uokik [Accessed 20 May 2025].

did not "roll" loans to hide arrears, but rather utilised legal loan rescheduling under the National Credit Act (NCA) to help stressed clients lower their monthly premiums by extending the repayment terms. Crucially, Capitec demonstrated that they did not charge new initiation fees on rescheduled loans and maintained strict provisioning rules for them. Ultimately, the SARB and independent financial analysts backed Capitec, concluding that Viceroy had misconstrued regular, transparent retail banking restructuring for illegal loan sharking practices.

Capitec have indicated that the bank's surplus capital may be deployed to support AvaFin's growth. The implication is significant: South African deposits, raised under a South African banking licence and protected within the country's banking supervisory framework, are now being used to fund online consumer lending in Mexico, Spain, Poland, Czechia, and Latvia — markets in which AvaFin's reported default rates exceed 50% of all loans issued [based on February 2026 results]. The transmission of risk from these markets to the South African retail depositor is unusual in modern South African banking practice. A pensioner in Mthatha now has indirect exposure to political and economic conditions in jurisdictions she has never heard of. Latvia, to take one example, borders Russia and has been, since 2022, on the frontline of NATO's eastern flank. The premium being earned in these markets is a function of the risk being underwritten. The depositor is not the party earning the premium, but they are arguably the party taking the risk.

AvaFin's balance sheet at year-end 2024 carried €45.2 million of equity against €142.1 million of total assets and over €71 million of borrowings — an equity ratio of approximately 32%. Against default rates of the magnitude reported, the equity buffer is not generous. Any adverse movement in collection performance, regulation, or local credit conditions in the relevant jurisdictions would pressure the equity position quickly.[120] A recapitalisation, whether from Capitec or from third-party debt, is the likely path of resolution for any such pressure. Capitec's surplus capital, generated from South African retail banking and insurance, is the most obvious source. When a public giant like Capitec takes total ownership of a private holding entity, the subsidiary is no longer required to publish standalone, public-facing annual reports. So unfortunately, we have not had site of the full financials for AvaFin since 2025, but presume that this recapitalisation has already occurred.

The book leaves much unsaid about what comes next. Capitec is likely to continue delivering strong reported growth over the next several years. The structural risks identified in earlier chapters — the loan book concentration, the recoveries-treatment legacy, the insurance correlation, the foreign lending exposure — will resolve themselves over time, in the direction the analytical framework would predict or against it. The opacity that has accompanied the bank's growth has two specific instruments. The first is the cell captive structure used historically for credit life insurance, which has limited public disclosure relative to fully-licensed underwriting. The second, newer, is the foreign subsidiary in AvaFin, whose accounts are not consolidated into Capitec's South African disclosures in the same form. Neither instrument is improper in itself. Both reduce the visibility of the underlying earnings composition to the reader of Capitec's primary financial statements.

[120] See 2024 AFS of AvaFin

The connections between Capitec and Steinhoff, established in earlier chapters of this book, are not coincidental. They are the visible surface of the network the third chapter described: the overlapping directorships, the shared Stellenbosch institutional history, the patterns of mutual support among men who have known each other for decades. The Steinhoff fraud is now in the public record. The Capitec story is not. Whether the two end up being told as comparable cautionary tales, or as a cautionary tale and its near-miss counterpart, is a question the next decade will have to answer.

Numbers, however polished, remain open to interpretation. The Capitec story is not solely about the bank. It is also about the market that has consistently rewarded the bank's growth, the JSE that has hosted its disclosures, the regulators who have defended its reporting, and the investors whose returns have depended on the bank's continued success.

Bankers who behave badly rarely change. The institutions that enable them change more slowly still. Trust, once lost, is difficult to regain — yet the market extends it again, persuaded by the next iteration of growth, innovation, and opportunity.

The clearest measure of how Capitec has changed is the average loan size. In 2014, the year African Bank collapsed, the average Capitec loan was R6,004, with a term of just under two years. By 2018 the average had climbed to R7,168, with terms extending to just over three years. By 2022, gross loans and advances stood at R108.8 billion and the personal loan book at R85.4 billion — and the average loan size, depending on the cohort measured, was between R65,615 and R85,692. The order of magnitude is the point. The average Capitec loan in 2022 was approximately ten times the size of the average loan in 2014, on terms that had also extended significantly.

Across the same period, the bank's credit client base remained relatively stable at around 1.2 million customers. The growth in the loan book has come from extending more credit to the same customers, on longer terms, through new products. The credit card was launched in September 2016. The Access Facility — the revolving credit product that allows a customer to repay the minimum and immediately redraw the same amount — was launched in May 2020. These products do not eliminate default risk. They defer its recognition. The personal loan book becomes a treadmill: the customer is always paying and always borrowing, the balance does not fall, and the moment of default is pushed indefinitely into the future. Until it isn't.

It is not the role of an author, nor of an auditor, to determine whether an unsecured loan book of this magnitude is too risky for the depositors and shareholders who carry the consequences. The auditor's role is to test whether the loan book is fairly stated under the applicable accounting standards. On forward-looking estimates — expected credit losses, recoveries assumptions, fair value of insurance liabilities — the standards permit, and in some cases require, significant deference to management judgement. The directors making those judgements are remunerated on the bank's reported performance. The investors who hold the shares are remunerated on the same performance. The depositors who fund the loan book are not parties to either compensation structure. They bear the risk. They do not earn the upside and they hope that *this time, it will be different*

30. Banker Bonuses

The earlier chapters of this book examined what Capitec does. The chapter on Viceroy Research described the gap between the reported loan book and what could be reconciled from disclosed numbers. The chapter on regulatory protection described how that gap was defended rather than examined. The chapter on insurance described how the bank's earnings diversification was, on the underlying risk, less diversified than the line-item disclosure suggested. The chapter on AvaFin described how South African deposits were now funding online lending in jurisdictions with default rates above 50%. The pattern across all of these chapters was the same: the bank's reported performance, on close reading, reflects accounting and product choices made by management, and the choices have consistently favoured higher reported earnings over more conservative recognition.

This chapter is about the people who make those choices, and how they are paid.

The analytical chain is short. Under the accounting standards Capitec has applied since 2019, loans are classified into stages. Stage 1 loans require small provisions. Stage 2 loans require substantially larger ones. The trigger for moving a loan from Stage 1 to Stage 2 is what the standards call a Significant Increase in Credit Risk — SICR. The standards do not define "significant" numerically. They leave the definition to management. At Capitec, the trigger for pre-arrears migration is anchored to a proprietary internal behaviour score, calibrated on Capitec's own data, reviewed annually by Capitec's own management, with no external benchmark disclosed. The four major South African banks anchor their SICR triggers at least partly to externally observable measures — credit bureau data, observable default rates, the universal IFRS 9 backstop of thirty days past due. Capitec does not.

Why this matters is mechanical. A small movement in where the behaviour score threshold sits can shift a meaningful number of loans between Stage 1 and Stage 2. The threshold itself is set by the same management whose reported earnings — and whose share-price-linked compensation — depend on the result. The auditor tests whether the model produces outputs consistent with the criteria. The auditor does not, and under the standards is not required to, test whether the threshold is set at an appropriate level. The dial that controls the impairment charge is held by the people whose pay depends on the impairment charge.

This is the chapter's central question. It is not whether executives at Capitec are paid too much in absolute terms — that argument is harder to make than the bank's critics often suppose, and the chapter will deal with it on its own merits. The deeper question is whether the structure of executive pay at Capitec rewards the same management discretion that the bank's accounting is built around. The two questions — what is the loan book worth, and what should the executives be paid — are not separable. They depend on each other, mechanically, by way of the share price.

The question is not a new one. Fourteen years before the events this chapter describes, the United States Congress passed legislation specifically designed to address it. The legislation has never been fully implemented. In July 2024, the U.S. Senator who had led the push for that legislation questioned the Federal Reserve Chairman on why.

Tuesday, 9 July 2024: Washington, D.C.

"Back in 2010, Congress passed the Dodd-Frank Act. Section 956 instructed financial regulators to address the issue of CEOs of giant banks increasing their bonuses by encouraging the banks to take on more risk. They run the risk of ending up like the banks that ran into trouble in 2008 and again in 2023. In 2018, you told this committee, Mr. Chairman, that you, I quote, "expect that banks will have in place compensation plans that do not provide incentives for excessive risk taking." In other words, you trusted the banks to write their own rules. Chair Powell, in the six-and-a-half years since you said to trust the banks to regulate themselves, how many of the ten biggest banks have put policies in place to delay annual bonuses for this broader group of critical employees whose risk-taking could endanger the bank?" U.S. Senator Elizabeth Warren was just getting started with her heated questioning.

"I don't know specifically, but my guess is all of them since the financial crisis," was the sheepish reply offered by Jerome Powell, the somewhat uncomfortable-looking Chairman of the Federal Reserve.

Peering over her spectacles from her perch above Powell, Warren's stern lambasting continued: "So, you're the regulator who said trust the banks to self-regulate so we can avoid another financial meltdown or another bailout, and you don't know if they did or didn't do that?"

"Well, you make— that's a very, very specific, narrow question you're asking," Powell replied while visibly uncomfortable shifting in his seat.

"No, it is a very specific thing because it's something a regulator should do. You think the answer is 10-out-of-10? The answer is zero out of ten," Senator Warren shouted back at him.

"Yeah, I doubt that," Powell shifted a little in his seat as he responded.

"Well, go back and look," the tense exchange continued. "So look, Chair Powell, the Fed has now refused to join the other financial regulators in finalising a rule implementing section 956, as Congress directed. *Dodd-Frank* was passed 14 years ago. There are still no rules to stop banks from rewarding executives' risky behaviour. When you were asked about these Section 956 rules—or lack of rules—in March of this year, you said that you wanted to "understand the problem we're solving before proposing a rule."

"Chair Powell, the law does not say: Jerome Powell, in his infinite wisdom, should decide if we have a problem with executive compensation." Holding no punches, Warren raised her voice as she continued, "The law, passed 14 years ago, says executive pay is a problem that threatens the stability of our economy, so write the rules to rein them in.

Warren lowered her voice as she began to wrap up the dressing-down, "Chair Powell, I understand why the ten biggest banks in the country like your approach. You let them do whatever they want, but you don't work for the giant banks. You work for the American people. I urge you to do your job. Thank you, Mr. Chairman."[121]

[121] An extract from a Press Release located on Elizabeth Warren's website. Available at: www.warren.senate.gov/newsroom/press-releases/at-hearing-warren-slams-powel-for-cozying-up-to-big-banks-and-inaction-on-executive-compensation-reform-calls-for-rulemaking-that-protects-stability-of-the-american-economy#:~:text=In%20a%20heated%20exchange%2C%20Senator,compensation%20reforms%20in%20place%2C%20Chair Accessed on: 10 July 2024

31. Appreciation Rights

In Capitec's gleaming Stellenbosch headquarters, a screen displays the company's share price for all to see, like a digital deity demanding constant attention. It's the scoreboard for the most expensive game in South African banking, where executives have turned their compensation into a high-stakes bet.

The share price determines executive compensation through the instrument by which most executive compensation is paid. That instrument is a Share Appreciation Right, or SAR, and Capitec's executive remuneration has been built on it for most of the bank's listed life.

A Share Appreciation Right is not a share. It is a contract. The executive is granted, at a specific date, a notional position in a specific number of shares at the prevailing share price. The grant requires no capital from the executive. The executive does not own the shares, does not vote them, and does not receive dividends on them. At a future date — typically three to five years after the grant, subject to performance conditions — the executive may exercise the rights. On exercise, the executive receives the difference between the share price on the exercise date and the share price on the grant date, in cash or in shares. If the share price has fallen below the grant price, the right expires worthless. If the share price has risen substantially, the executive receives substantial value without ever having put any capital at risk.

The instrument is widespread in modern listed-company remuneration and is not, in itself, controversial. It allows the company to offer significant performance-linked compensation without requiring executives to hold equity they may not be able to afford. It aligns, in the conventional formulation, the executive's interests with those of the shareholder.

The conventional formulation depends, however, on the executive being a price-taker rather than a price-maker. The shareholder benefits when the share price rises because the share price reflects, however imperfectly, the underlying performance of the business. The executive whose pay is linked to the share price has every incentive to maximise the underlying business performance, because ultimately that is the only mechanism by which the share price rises over a sustained period of time.

The previous chapter described the mechanism by which a Capitec executive can also influence the reported underlying performance directly. The threshold at which a loan migrates from Stage 1 to Stage 2 is set by management. The impairment charge depends on that migration. The earnings depend on the impairment charge. The share price depends on the earnings. The SAR pays out on the share price. Each link in that chain is individually defensible. Together they describe a remuneration structure in which the people who determine the inputs are paid on the output.

Gerrie Fourie served as Capitec's chief executive officer from 2014 until his retirement in 2025. Over the eight years from 2017 to 2025, his cumulative compensation was approximately R529 million. Of that, roughly R224 million came in cash — salaries, short-term incentives, and other annual cash payments. The remaining R305 million came from long-term incentives, the substantial majority of which were SARs. For the year to February 2025 alone, Fourie's total compensation was R104.8 million, of which R75 million came from SAR vesting in a year when Capitec's share price rose 52%. The remuneration report for that year described the share-price performance as having produced "above-target" payments to executives.

These figures, taken in isolation, are not extraordinary by the standards of South African banking remuneration. Nedbank's chief executive Jason Quinn received R119.7 million in 2024, in a year when Nedbank's earnings grew 3%. Standard Bank's senior executives operate within similar ranges. The South African banking sector is well-paid by the standards of the country's broader economy and approximately average by the standards of international banking. If the argument were simply that Fourie was paid too much, the argument would not be particularly strong.

The argument is not that Fourie was paid too much. The argument is that he was paid for outcomes he himself helped determine.

The structural feature of Capitec's remuneration framework that distinguishes it from those of the other major South African banks is what the SAR is anchored to. The SAR pays on the share price. The share price responds to reported earnings. The reported earnings depend in part on the impairment charge. The impairment charge depends in part on the SICR threshold. The SICR threshold is set by Capitec's management, anchored to a proprietary internal behaviour score that no external party can independently calibrate. The other major banks anchor their SICR triggers at least partly to externally observable measures. Capitec does not.

This is the system that produces a R305 million long-term incentive payout over eight years. The payout is mathematically valid — the share price did rise, the SARs were exercised at the higher price, the difference was paid. The validity of the calculation is not in dispute. What is in dispute, or should be, is whether the inputs to the share price reflect underlying performance independent of management discretion, or whether they reflect, in part, the same management discretion that is being compensated by the resulting share-price movement.

The bank's own remuneration disclosures address this question only at the highest level. Performance conditions for SAR vesting include return on equity, earnings growth, and the Customer Satisfaction score. The first two are derived from the financial statements whose accounting choices are made by the same executives whose SARs are vesting. The third is defined, measured, and reported by Capitec's own management, with no externally benchmarked alternative disclosed. The Nedbank remuneration framework uses an externally benchmarked client satisfaction metric for the equivalent purpose. Capitec uses its own.

There is one further feature of Capitec's executive shareholdings that has received less attention than it should.

In the COVID-19 market crash of March 2020, Capitec's share price fell from over R1,300 to an intraday low of R539 — a 58% decline in a matter of weeks. The collapse was severe enough that the bank issued a SENS announcement explaining the mechanics of what had happened. The explanation was that algorithmic selling had been triggered by the share price breaking through a "put strike price" associated with a collar structure held by the founder, Michiel Le Roux. The collar — a derivative structure combining a purchased put option with a sold call option — had been arranged by Le Roux through entities named Limietberg and Kalander, with Goldman Sachs as the counterparty. As the share price fell through the put strike, the structure's hedging requirements triggered automatic selling that accelerated the decline.

The founder of Capitec — the man whose name is synonymous with the bank's culture, whose public statements describe Capitec as a long-term franchise built on conservative principles, and who serves as the bank's symbolic standard-bearer for the long view — had personally paid Goldman Sachs to insure himself against a decline in the bank's share price. The collar structure caps Le Roux's upside above a certain strike (in 2024 disclosures, between R4,437 and R4,477) in exchange for downside protection below another strike (between R2,424 and R2,498). Le Roux is, in effect, willing to forgo significant additional gains in exchange for protection against significant losses.

A founder may have many reasons for hedging a concentrated personal position. Tax planning, estate planning, diversification, the desire to fund non-Capitec investments without selling Capitec shares — all of these are legitimate. The hedge is not, by itself, evidence of anything other than prudent personal financial management.

It is, however, an interesting signal. The executives whose pay is determined by the share price hold SARs, which pay out only if the share price rises. However, notwithstanding the drop in share price in 2021, the executive still paid themselves, stating the share price fall as an anomaly outside of their control. The founder, whose existing wealth is determined by the share price, holds a structure that protects him against the share price falling. The executives have, in effect, been given the upside of the share price without the downside. The founder has bought the downside protection out of his own pocket. The depositors and minority shareholders have neither the upside instrument nor the downside hedge.

Fourie's compensation, taken on its own terms, is within the range of South African banking peers and is not the substance of the criticism. The substance is that the bank's remuneration design rewards exactly the management discretion that the bank's accounting framework relies upon. This is not unique to Capitec — variations of the same problem exist across the banking sector globally, which is why the United States Congress, fourteen years before the writing of this chapter, passed legislation specifically aimed at it. The legislation has not been fully implemented in the United States, and no equivalent legislation has been introduced in South Africa.

The system works in the sense that it produces the outcomes it is designed to produce. The share price rises. The executives are compensated. The reported earnings support both. The structural question is what happens when the share price does not rise.

The COVID crash was the closest the bank has come, in its listed history, to testing that question. The price fell 58% over a few weeks. The recovery began within days, supported in part by management's own purchases at the lows. By the end of the financial year the position had largely been restored. The SARs that were unvested at the bottom would, on their normal vesting schedules, have been measured against a recovering price. The SARs that vested at the bottom were a smaller share of the total.

The next test of the system is the one that has not yet occurred. The share price has continued to rise. The SARs have continued to vest at higher levels. The remuneration figures have continued to grow. The mathematics is, for now, working in the same direction it has worked in for most of the bank's listed life. The question the chapter raises is not whether the mathematics is wrong. The question is whether the mathematics is independent of the management whose pay depends on it. What still needs to be tested, to a larger degree, is what happens when the share price moves the other way.

32. Banking Failure

The third chapter of this book proposed that banks fail for three reasons, and only three. They lose money on the loans they make. They lose the confidence of their depositors. Or they are run by people who are not up to the job. The framework was first applied to the goldsmith-banks brought down by Charles II in 1672. It has applied to every banking failure since. It is the framework against which the rest of this book has been written.

The chapter has now come back to itself. The book has spent thirty chapters documenting how Capitec was built, how it has been managed, how its accounting has been structured, how its insurance has grown, how its foreign exposure has been arranged, and how its executives have been paid. The question that closes the book is the one chapter three opened it with: where, in this institution, would failure come from if it came?

Before answering, the scale needs to be established. Capitec is not the bank some of its critics imagine it to be. At the end of February 2025 it carried total assets of R238.5 billion[122] and equity of R50.9 billion. Those are meaningful absolute numbers. They are also, by the standards of the South African banking sector, modest. FirstRand carries total assets of R2.5 trillion and equity of R229.9 billion. Standard Bank carries R3.2 trillion and R292.7 billion. ABSA carries R2 trillion and R183.3 billion. Nedbank, the smallest of the Big Four, carries R1.3 trillion and

[122] Year end June 2024 fo Firstrand and December 2024 for the other banks.

R90 billion. Capitec's total assets are roughly a tenth of Standard Bank's. Its equity is a fifth of Nedbank's.

Where Capitec leads its peers is in ratios rather than absolutes. Its equity-to-asset ratio of approximately 21% is the highest in South African banking by a significant margin. Its return on equity is the highest in the sector. Its return on assets is the highest in the sector. These are real strengths and the chapter does not seek to diminish them. They are also, on a closer reading, partly a consequence of what Capitec does not do. The bank holds almost no mortgage book. It holds almost no corporate book of any meaningful size. Its lending is short-duration, unsecured, retail and increasingly insurance-correlated. The capital intensity of its business is lower than that of its peers because the regulatory capital charges against its specific mix of assets are lower. The high ROE is not a free gift of management quality. It is, in part, the arithmetic consequence of a particular kind of balance sheet.

African Bank, at the point of its 2014 collapse, held approximately 2% of South African banking assets. Roughly R43 billion of unsecured loans were at risk. The collapse was not caused by African Bank being large. It was caused by impairment losses exceeding the bank's ability to absorb them. The lesson is that the absolute size of a bank tells you something about its systemic importance and almost nothing about its likelihood of failure. The lesson recurs in the global record. Credit Suisse held $574 billion in total assets when it failed in 2023. Silicon Valley Bank held $209 billion when it failed in the same month. Lehman

Brothers held more than $600 billion at its collapse in 2008. Larger banks have failed in greater absolute numbers than smaller ones, because the larger ones tend to be more leveraged, more exposed to wholesale funding, and more interconnected with the rest of the financial system.

Capitec's size is not its protection. Nor is it its problem. The question is what the bank holds and how it is run. The three-causes framework applies in turn.

The chapters of this book have argued that Capitec's loan book is more concentrated, more correlated, and more dependent on management discretion than the headline disclosures suggest. The book is almost entirely unsecured. The customer base is overwhelmingly South African, overwhelmingly lower-income, and structurally exposed to the same economic conditions that determine credit life insurance claims. The Access Facility and its predecessor products allow customers to repay arrears and immediately redraw the same amount, deferring the recognition of default. The SICR threshold that determines when a loan is migrated from stage 1 to stage 2 is anchored to a proprietary internal score set by the same management whose compensation depends on the resulting impairment charge.

The bank reports stage 3 loans of roughly 11% to 13% of the gross book in recent years. By the standards of international retail banking, where stage 3 ratios of 2% to 4% are typical, this is high. The bank's provisioning against these loans is substantial, and the coverage ratio has been maintained at levels that would, in a stable economic environment, be sufficient. The question the framework asks is what happens to the provisioning if the assumptions on which it rests are tested by an environment less stable than the one in which they were calibrated.

The bank's expected credit loss model is sophisticated, internally consistent, and entirely dependent on inputs that Capitec's management generates and Capitec's management interprets. The auditor tests the model for internal consistency. The auditor does not, under the applicable standards, independently calibrate the model's assumptions. The loan book's reported quality is, in the end, what management says it is. The depositors, the minority shareholders, and the public are dependent on the integrity of that judgement. The book has not argued that the judgement has been dishonest. It has argued that the judgement is unverifiable from the outside, that the incentive structure rewards aggressive judgement over conservative judgement, and that aggressive judgement, sustained for long enough, produces outcomes indistinguishable from honest deterioration in the underlying book.

The Viceroy report of 2018 raised these questions and was rebutted in a way that did not address the questions it had actually raised. The gap between Capitec's reported loan book and what could be reconciled from external information was approximately R3 billion in 2017, building toward the R950 million reduction in retained earnings that the bank ultimately took on adopting IFRS 9 in 2019. The Viceroy report had identified the gap correctly. The mechanism the report attributed to the gap was wrong. The bank's defence focused on the wrong mechanism. The right mechanism — the recognition of estimated future recoveries within the gross loan book under the prior accounting standard — was disclosed in the footnotes and not addressed by the public defence. The same pattern of disclosure has continued under IFRS 9 in a different form, with the SICR threshold doing the work that the recoveries treatment did before.

If Capitec fails through the first cause, it will fail because the cumulative effect of years of aggressive judgement, compounding inside a loan book whose true quality has been progressively obscured by product design and accounting choice, will exceed the bank's capacity to absorb the consequences. The capital adequacy ratio of 33% provides a substantial buffer. The buffer is sufficient against the kinds of losses that have historically been recognised. Whether it is sufficient against the kinds of losses that have not yet been recognised is a different question, and one that cannot be answered from outside the bank.

Capitec's deposit base is large, broad, and structurally retail. The bank funds itself primarily through the savings and transactional accounts of its 24 million customers, with comparatively little reliance on wholesale funding. This is, in conventional analysis, a source of significant strength. Retail deposits are stickier than wholesale funding. They are protected, up to specified limits, by the deposit insurance scheme established under recent legislation. They are spread across millions of individual accounts, no single one of which is material to the bank's liquidity position.

These factors reduce the probability of a deposit run. They do not eliminate it. Modern deposit runs do not require depositors to queue physically outside a branch. The 2023 collapse of Silicon Valley Bank was, in operational terms, a smartphone-driven run that completed faster than any equivalent event in banking history — a quarter of the bank's deposit base withdrew within a single trading day. The technology that allows Capitec's customers to manage their accounts in real time, on their phones, with no friction, is the same technology that would allow them to withdraw their balances in real time, on their phones, with no friction, in the event of a confidence shock.

The confidence shock that would trigger such an event is not currently visible. The bank's public profile is strong. Its regulatory relationships are good. The South African Reserve Bank has, on the public record, intervened to defend the bank against critical reporting on more than one occasion. The kind of triggering event that would matter would have to be substantial enough to overcome both the bank's own communications response and the regulatory backstop. The book has not predicted such an event. It has documented the structural features that would make the consequences of such an event more severe than the surface metrics imply: the customer base's economic vulnerability, the loan book's correlation with the same economic conditions that would drive the run, and the insurance book's further correlation with both.

This is the cause the book has examined in most detail, and it is the cause for which the framework provides the least comforting reading.

The chapters of this book have documented, with reference to public records, court filings, regulatory disclosures, and the bank's own annual reports: an accounting treatment that supported earnings for nearly a decade and was discontinued only when the accounting standards made continuation impossible; a regulatory response to critical research that was rapid, well-resourced, and substantially in the bank's favour; an insurance growth strategy that diversifies the income statement without diversifying the underlying risk; a foreign expansion that exposes South African depositors to the credit conditions of jurisdictions with reported default rates above 40%; and a remuneration structure in which the people setting the dials that determine reported earnings are paid in instruments whose value depends on those same earnings.

Each of these, taken alone, is defensible. Each has been defended by the bank's management and by its supporters in commentary and in parliament. Taken together, they describe an institution in which the formal rules of banking — capital adequacy, audit, disclosure, regulatory supervision — are observed with care, and in which the informal rules described in chapter three remain operative beneath them. The accounting choices are within the standards. The remuneration is within market norms. The insurance growth is within the regulatory framework. The foreign expansion is within the SARB's approval.

None of the individual choices is improper. The pattern of choices is what the book has been about.

If Capitec fails through the third cause, it will not fail because of a single bad decision. It will fail because a pattern of decisions, each individually defensible, has cumulatively produced an institution whose underlying risk is greater than its reported metrics suggest — and because the same management whose pattern of decisions produced the gap is also the management responsible for closing it. The auditors test the standards. The standards permit the discretion. The discretion has been exercised consistently in one direction. The direction has been favourable for the share price. The share price has been favourable for the executives. The executives are the people who exercise the discretion.

At the time of writing, Capitec trades at approximately R3,500 per share, with a price-to-book ratio of roughly eight times. The other South African banks trade at price-to-book ratios of between one and two times. The African banking sector averages below one. The global retail banking sector averages around one. Capitec's valuation is, by every reasonable comparator, an outlier.

A valuation of this magnitude reflects the market's view that Capitec will continue to deliver growth and returns that no other comparable institution can match. The view may be correct. The book has not argued that the bank will fail. It has argued that the conditions for failure are structurally present in the institution, that the regulatory and reporting environment has consistently obscured rather than illuminated those conditions, and that the gap between the bank's reported risk and its underlying risk has been growing for years.

A price-to-book ratio of eight means that for every rand of tangible equity the bank holds, the market is paying eight rands. The remaining seven rands represent the market's confidence that future earnings will sustain a return on equity high enough to justify the premium indefinitely. That confidence is now larger, in valuation terms, than the bank's entire capital base. A 50% reduction in the price-to-book multiple, to a level still well above the South African peer average, would represent a destruction of investor wealth of approximately R150 billion. A reversion to peer multiples would represent destruction of close to the bank's entire market capitalisation.

None of this requires the bank to fail. It requires only that the market's view of the bank's future earnings reverts to something resembling the view it takes of comparable institutions.

Banks fail for three reasons. They lose money on loans, their depositors leave, or they are run by people who are not up to the job. The first cause requires the underlying loan book to be worse than the reported loan book, sustained for long enough that the gap exceeds the bank's capital buffer. The second cause requires a confidence shock large enough to overcome the bank's response and the regulator's defence. The third cause requires nothing dramatic at all. It requires only that the people running the bank continue to make the kinds of decisions they have been making, in the same direction they have been making them, until the cumulative consequence of the decisions becomes unmanageable.

The first cause is plausible and not currently visible. The second is unlikely and not currently visible. The third is documented across this book and is the cause that the framework was originally designed to capture. Charles II did not lose his goldsmith-bankers because of a single bad loan or a sudden run on deposits. He lost them because the political and economic structures around the Crown's borrowing made the goldsmiths' position unsustainable in ways the goldsmiths themselves could not control. The structures of South African banking are not the structures of seventeenth-century English public finance. The principle is the same. Institutions that depend, beneath their formal frameworks, on the continued cooperation of a small network of people whose interests align with one another more than with the institution's depositors will eventually encounter a circumstance in which the cooperation cannot be sustained.

This book has been an attempt to describe that network, the institution it built, and the structural features that make the framework relevant. The market will, in the end, reach its own conclusion. The depositors will reach theirs. The regulators will reach theirs. The author has reached his.

33. Misplaced Loyalty

Markus Jooste took his own life on 22 March 2024, on a coastal path near his home in Hermanus. He had been the chief executive of Steinhoff International until his resignation in December 2017, when the company's auditors refused to sign off on its financial statements and the share price collapsed. The day before his death, the Financial Sector Conduct Authority had imposed an administrative penalty of R475 million in respect of his role in the Steinhoff fraud. The penalty was a fraction of the estimated R106 billion loss that the fraud had ultimately produced for Steinhoff shareholders, creditors, and counterparties.

His death closed more than a personal account.

The PwC investigation into Steinhoff had documented, over the years following the collapse, a fraud involving fictitious profits of approximately €6.5 billion across more than a decade of reported earnings. The investigation's findings had been substantially sealed and would not, in their fullest form, be made public. The criminal proceedings that had been progressing slowly through the German and South African justice systems would not now proceed against Jooste personally. The civil litigation against his estate would continue, on different terms and against different defendants. The witnesses who would have been compelled to testify against him in his presence would now testify, if at all, in his absence. The questions that he alone could have answered would not be answered. The first rule of the network described in the third chapter of this book — ons praat nie uit nie — became, in his case, permanent.

This is the structural feature of the South African corporate landscape that this book has been about. Not the specific accounting choices, the specific lending products, the specific remuneration structures — although the book has documented all of those. The deeper feature is the one that becomes visible at moments like this: the manner in which accountability, when it finally arrives, tends to arrive too late, or to arrive against the wrong defendants, or to arrive against an estate rather than a person, or not to arrive at all. The institutions remain. The questions remain. The people who could have answered them are not always available when the questions are being asked.

The clearest illustration of how the network closes itself around its own collapse is the story of Christo Wiese.

Wiese had been one of South Africa's most successful businessmen for forty years before he encountered Markus Jooste. He had built Pep Stores and Shoprite into dominant retail operations. He had survived the Tollgate collapse with his personal position intact. He had navigated the political transition of 1994 better than most of his Afrikaner business peers. His commercial judgement, by any reasonable measure, was among the sharpest in South African corporate life.

It was Wiese who, in 2014, exchanged his controlling interest in Pepkor for Steinhoff shares. It was Wiese who, the same year, exchanged his KWV holdings for additional Steinhoff stock. It was

Wiese who took Lanzerac, sold it to him a generation earlier in disputed circumstances, and traded it to Jooste for ten million Steinhoff shares. By the time Steinhoff collapsed in December 2017, Wiese was its largest individual shareholder. His personal losses from the collapse, on his own subsequent claim, exceeded R59 billion.

The warning had been delivered before any of the exchanges were complete. Whitey Basson, who had built Shoprite alongside Wiese over decades and who knew both men well, told Wiese directly that he was "trading a champion horse for a donkey." Basson said this on the record. Wiese has not, to my knowledge, disputed that Basson said it. Wiese proceeded with the exchanges anyway.

This is not a story about a businessman who failed to do his due diligence. Wiese had access to information about Steinhoff that no outside investor possessed. He sat on the company's supervisory board. He had known Jooste for decades. They shared the same Stellenbosch institutional history that this book has documented in earlier chapters. They had built businesses together. They had funded each other's ventures. They had vouched for each other in front of regulators and journalists. The exchanges that destroyed approximately R59 billion of Wiese's personal wealth were not made in spite of his relationship with Jooste. They were made because of it.

Wiese eventually settled with Steinhoff in 2022 for approximately R7 billion in cash and a 5% stake in Pepkor, applying the legal principle that fraud voids contracts from the outset. He recovered some of what he had lost. He did not recover most of it. He emerged, as he had emerged from earlier controversies in his career, financially intact and reputationally diminished. His commercial judgement — the sharpest in South African corporate life — had been catastrophically wrong on one specific question, and the question had been about whether he could trust a man whose interests had appeared to align with his own.

If this kind of misplaced loyalty can destroy the position of the most sophisticated businessman in the country, the structural problem this book has identified does not require the leadership of any specific institution to be incompetent or dishonest. It requires only that the leadership be embedded in the same network as the people who would do them, or their depositors, eventual harm. The auditors test the standards. The standards permit the discretion. The discretion is exercised by people who are, in many cases, members of the same network as the people who would, in another version of events, be holding them to account.

The regulatory apparatus has done what it could in the years since Steinhoff. The Financial Sector Conduct Authority has expanded its enforcement powers and has, with some inconsistency, applied them. The South African Reserve Bank has continued to defend the institutions under its supervision. Parliament has held hearings, received briefings, and produced reports. The Corporation for Deposit Insurance, which commenced operations on 1 April 2024, now protects retail and non-financial private depositors up to R100,000 per depositor per bank, with target reimbursement within twenty calendar days. The CODI scheme is a meaningful protection for ordinary South African depositors and represents one of the more substantive post-2017 regulatory reforms.

The R100,000 threshold is the floor. Above the floor, the depositor is an unsecured creditor of the institution. A pensioner with a R500,000 fixed deposit at a South African bank is protected, by CODI, for the first R100,000 of that balance. The remaining R400,000 depends entirely on the continued solvency of the institution. For the South African retail depositor whose balance exceeds the CODI threshold — the depositor in possession of meaningful savings, the small business owner with operating capital, the household with a deposit against a future home purchase — the protection ends where the protection ends. Beyond that, the depositor is responsible for understanding what is being done with the money.

This book has tried to provide a framework for that understanding. The framework is the one the third chapter set out. There are two rules of the game in South African banking. The first rule is written into the Banks Act, the Basel accords, and the audited financial statements. It says that institutions must hold capital, manage liquidity, disclose performance, and submit to audit. It is the rule the regulator monitors and the public reads. The second rule is older. It is taught in residences and reinforced in churches and applied across decades of business relationships. It says that the people running these institutions are members of networks whose loyalties precede their formal duties and whose obligations sometimes operate against the interests of the depositors, the minority shareholders, and the public. Both rules operate simultaneously. The first is visible. The second is not.

The framework also names the three causes of banking failure. Loan defaults. Deposit runs. Poor management. These are the only three causes there have ever been. They have applied to every banking collapse since 1672 and they will apply to every banking collapse that follows. The earlier chapters of this book have applied them to Capitec specifically. Whether the application proves correct, in the sense that Capitec eventually fails, is a question this book cannot answer. The book has not predicted the bank's failure. It has documented the structural conditions under which failure becomes more likely, and the gap between those conditions and the metrics by which the bank is currently valued.

The market will reach its own conclusion in time. The regulators will reach theirs. The depositors will reach theirs, individually and severally, as they decide what to do with their savings. The author has reached his, which is recorded in the foregoing pages. The reader is now in possession of the same framework the author has used to reach it, and is invited to apply it as the reader sees fit.

Banks are designed to fail. They are expected to fail. They will fail.

The only question that has ever mattered is which one, and when.

A note on what comes next

The framework this book has used to examine Capitec — the two rules of the game, the three causes of failure, the gap between the formal apparatus of banking regulation and the institutional reality beneath it — was developed for a study of a specific bank in a specific country. The framework also has broader application.

The next book in this sequence, ***Where Money Goes to Die,*** *applies the same scepticism to a larger question: what happens to banking, and to the broader financial system, as the legitimacy of government-issued currency comes under sustained pressure for the first time in a century. Bitcoin is the worked example. The same questions about who is trusted with what, and on what basis, recur in a different form. The same questions about differentiating between value and price, between what is authentic and what is artificial are asked and answered.*

The reader who has found the argument of this book useful is invited to indulge in a blend of literary fiction with literary non-fiction with Michael Saylor and a Picasso painting as central figures to the narrative.

Acknowledgments

For igniting my obsession with unravelling the enigma around the three billion in extra funds in Capitec's loan book, I acknowledge *Fraser John Perring*. He also offered me support in a manner that I would not have expected, and for that I am eternally grateful.

TJ Strydom, for his well-researched, albeit slightly sanitised works that provoked and inspired me to consider the unsaid gaps between the numbers and the narrative[123] that I felt demanded a voice.

Michelle Botes (born 12 October 1962 - died 21 December 2024) was a motivator who inspired me to complete my writing journey, despite never being given the same opportunity to finish what she started.

None of this would have been possible without the agency afforded to me by those who allowed me to freely indulge in this obsession, sometimes at significant financial cost. For this, I would like to dedicate this book to *Cheré Martin*.

And finally, here is to all the bibliophiles.

---

[123] Strydom TJ (2024), Stalking Giants, Tafelberg | Strydom, TJ (2019), Christo Wiese Risk & Riches, Tafelberg

www.ingramcontent.com/pod-product-compliance
Lightning Source LLC
LaVergne TN
LVHW040518210926
848480LV00007BA/1505
* 9 7 8 1 0 3 7 0 4 0 4 2 9 *